ALL ABOUT
JESUS

The Single Story
from Matthew, Mark, Luke, and John

ALL ABOUT
JESUS

The Single Story
from Matthew, Mark, Luke, and John

Compiled by Roger Quy

Authentic

ATLANTA · LONDON · HYDERABAD

Authentic Publishing
We welcome your questions and comments.

USA	PO Box 444, 285 Lynnwood Ave, Tyrone, GA, 30290
	www.authenticbooks.com
UK	9 Holdom Avenue, Bletchley, Milton Keynes, Bucks, MK1 1QR, UK
	www.authenticmedia.co.uk
India	Logos Bhavan, Medchal Road, Jeedimetla Village, Secunderabad 500 055, A.P.

All About Jesus
ISBN-13: 978-1-932805-73-4
ISBN-10: 1-932805-73-7

Harmony of the Gospels, front and back study helps
© 2004 by R. Quy, Ph.D., the Harmony Trust.
Special thanks to Ron Youngblood, Ph.D., for assistance with the Introduction and to Gene
Rubingh, Ph.D., for theological guidance.

10 09 08 07 06 / 6 5 4 3 2 1

Published in 2007 by Authentic

Library of Congress Cataloging-in-Publication Data

Bible. N.T. Gospels. English. New International Reader's Version. 2007.
  All about Jesus : the single story from Matthew, Mark, Luke, and John.
     p. cm.
  Includes bibliographical references and index.
  ISBN 978-1-932805-73-4 (pbk.)
  1. Bible. N.T. Gospels--Harmonies, English. 2. Jesus Christ--Biography--Sources, Biblical. I. Authentic
Publishing. II. Title.

BS2553.N485 2007
226'.1--dc22
                          2006036996

Cover design: Kirk DouPonce, dogeareddesign.com
Interior design: Angela Lewis

Printed in the United States of America

CONTENTS

Places in the Life of Jesus vii
Introduction 1

Chapter

1	God Reaches Out	7
2	A Special Birth	15
3	Preparing the Way	23
4	Jesus Starts his Mission	29
5	Opposition Begins	39
6	Teaching the People	51
7	Accused of Using Evil	63
8	Calming a Storm	75
9	Feeding the Hungry Crowds	85
10	Seen in God's Glory	97
11	Claiming God's Name	107
12	Who Is He?	115
13	Raising the Dead	129
14	Welcomed as King	141
15	Authority Questioned	155
16	Talking About the Future	167
17	Betrayed by a Friend	177
18	Facing False Charges	195
19	Nailed to a Cross	205
20	Back from the Dead	211
21	More to Come	217

Chapter Notes 223
References 239

Places in the Life
of Jesus

With insert showing modern countries of the region

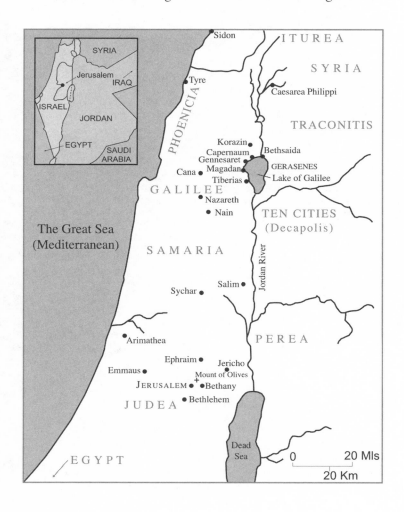

Introduction

Many people have questions about Jesus. Most people don't know much about him. They might only know what they have heard from others. But some want to find out more. They wonder if what Christians say about him is true. Can he really bring them peace? Can he bring them closer to God?

Jesus Christ was born in a small Jewish village 2,000 years ago. He was a carpenter until he was about 30 years old. Then he became a preacher and healer. He traveled less than 100 miles from his home. And his mission lasted no more than three years. He preached about God's love and performed many miracles. He attracted a large group of followers. But the religious leaders were afraid of him. So they arrested him and nailed him to a cross.

His followers claimed that he came back to life and returned to heaven. They believed in Jesus, even though many were put in jail or killed for following him. They became known as "Christians." And they spread his message throughout the world.

Why is Jesus so important?

Jesus Christ has affected history more than any other person. What he did changed the world forever. His followers are members of the world's largest religion. There are now almost two billion Christians around the world.

Jesus had a very important message. He talked about God and about life after death. He made some amazing claims about himself. Jesus said that he is "the one who came from heaven." He said, "God loved the world so much that he gave his one and only Son.... He sent his Son to save the world through him.... Then everyone who believes in him can live with God forever."

Many people have believed in Jesus. They have found his promises to be true. He has brought faith, hope and purpose to millions of people. Some people don't believe in Jesus Christ or try to live by his teachings. But they may call themselves Christians anyway. Millions of others say that they have come to know Jesus as a real friend. And he has changed their lives.

Jesus preached the good news about God's love for everyone. Yet some people did not believe his message. Jesus warned them. He said, "The words that you hear me say are not my own. They belong to the Father who sent me.... There is a judge for anyone who does not accept me and my words. The very words I have spoken will judge him on the last day."

How do we know about Jesus?

Accounts of Jesus' life were written not long after he died. They are called the "gospels." (Gospel comes from an old word that means good news.) These gospel accounts became part of the Christian Bible that we have today.

Some other Jewish and Roman writers also mention Jesus. Most history scholars of today agree that Jesus really did live 2,000 years ago.

There are four gospel accounts in the Bible. These are the gospels of Matthew, Mark, Luke and John. The gospel accounts came from reports by Jesus' followers and by others who knew him.

Jesus chose 12 of his many followers to travel with him. He

called that small group his disciples. The disciples gave personal reports about the things that Jesus said and did.

Matthew was one of the disciples. He collected taxes for the Romans before he met Jesus. Matthew's gospel was meant for Jewish people. It explains how the Jewish Scriptures told about who Jesus really is. This gospel connects the Old and New Testaments of the Bible.

Mark was a young man who followed Jesus. The first Christians met in his mother's house for prayer. Mark was not one of the disciples. But he helped Simon Peter, who was one of the disciples closest to Jesus. Mark's gospel is a short history of the life and message of Jesus.

Luke was a doctor who knew the disciples. Luke may have learned from Jesus' mother many of the things he wrote. Luke said that he had "carefully looked into everything from the beginning." Then he wrote "an orderly report of exactly what happened." Luke also wrote the book of Acts, which describes how the Christian church began.

John was another of the disciples. He was a fisherman before he met Jesus. Like Matthew, John traveled with Jesus and saw the things that Jesus did. John's gospel is about who Jesus really is and why he came. It explains that Jesus is God himself, who became a human being to show us what God is like and to die for our sins.

Bible scholars think that Mark's gospel was the earliest of the four, written in about A.D. 70. Matthew and Luke used most of Mark's gospel in their own gospels. They also used other writings that scholars believe came from a common source.

The gospels of Matthew, Mark and Luke are similar. But John's gospel is different from the others. It was written last, in about A.D. 95. It contains many details about Jesus that are not found in the other gospels.

Before the four gospels were written, the stories about Jesus were handed down by word of mouth. Most people were not able to read at the time of Jesus. So they remembered the sermons of well-

3

known preachers and passed them on. The reports of what Jesus said and did were told over and over again.

These reports were included in the gospels. Luke wrote, "Reports of these things were handed down to us. There were people who saw these things from the beginning and then passed the word on." Many of those people were still alive when the gospels were written.

The gospels were collected with other writings of the early church. This collection became known as the New Testament. The New Testament is all about the life and message of Jesus Christ. The Old Testament contains the Scriptures of the Jewish Bible.

The Christian Church carefully copied and saved the New Testament. We have more copies of the New Testament sources than of any other writings from that time in history.

Jesus and his disciples spoke Aramaic, the language of the Jewish people. But the gospel writers wrote in Greek, which was a common language of the Roman Empire.

The first English translation of the Greek New Testament was printed in the 16th century. The translation was brought up to date when older copies of the New Testament were found.

There are now many different translations of the Bible. Some are word-for-word translations. Others are more like a thought-for-thought translation. Some Bibles use elegant, old-fashioned language. Other Bibles use modern, everyday language. The most popular modern English translation of the Bible today is the New International Version® (NIV).

What is *All About Jesus*?

This book combines the four gospels into a single story. *All About Jesus* makes it easy to read a complete account of the life and message of Jesus Christ. None of the four gospels alone gives a complete picture of Jesus' life. Each gospel writer chose to highlight different things. This book brings together all the details from Matthew, Mark, Luke and John in one place.

The story uses the New International Reader's Version® (NIrV) of the Bible. This is an easy-to-read version of the popular NIV. The NIrV is meant for people who are reading the Bible for the first time.

The idea of putting the four gospel accounts into one is not new. A book like this was written as early as the second century. Many similar books have been written since. But this is the first to use the easy-to-read language of the NIrV.

This book uses only the text of the NIrV as much as possible. The story is woven together from the sentences of the gospels.

This book doesn't use the common chapter and verse divisions of the Bible. Scholars added these divisions to the Bible long after it was written.

It is not easy to fit the gospels together into a single story. The gospel writers had good reasons for their differences. These differences are lost in a single account.

Many decisions were needed to put the story together. Each gospel writer recorded different details. The point of the story was more important than the details of how, where and when it happened.

The gospel writers sometimes told about similar things happening at a different time or place. We don't always know whether these were different events or not. Jesus may have given the same message on more than one occasion. Several similar events are not repeated in this book.

Sometimes, when details in the gospels differ, the text found in two or more gospels was chosen. Otherwise, the gospel was chosen that helps you read the story better.

There is a list of Bible references at the end of this book. Events in the life of Jesus are listed in the same order as they appear in each chapter. You can use this list to find and compare each of the gospel accounts.

Some background details are given to help readers who are new to the Bible. These details are found in the chapter notes. The small numbers in the text mark these notes.

Jesus and the gospel writers often quoted from the Jewish Scriptures. The chapter notes include the Bible references for these quotations.

All About Jesus should not be used to replace the Bible. This book was written to bring the story of Jesus to those who otherwise might not read it. The purpose is to encourage people to read the Bible for themselves.

This book is meant for those who would like to find out more about Jesus. It is ideal for someone who is new to the Bible. Readers who already know the Bible may find that it helps them learn more about the life and message of Jesus.

chapter one

God Reaches Out

This is the beginning of the good news about Jesus Christ, the Son of God.

In the beginning, the Word[1] was already there. The Word was with God, and the Word was God. He was with God in the beginning.

All things were made through him. Nothing that has been made was made without him. Life was in him, and that life was the light for all people. The light shines in the darkness. But the darkness has not understood it. The true light that gives light to every man was coming into the world.

The Word was in the world that was made through him. But the world did not recognize him. He came to what was his own. But his own people did not accept him.

Some people did accept him. They believed in his name. He gave them the right to become children of God. To be a child of God has nothing to do with human parents. Children of God are not born because of human choice or because a husband wants them to be born. They are born because of what God does.

The Word became a human being. He made his home with us. We have seen his glory. It is the glory of the one and only Son.

He came from the Father. And he was full of grace and truth.

We have all received one blessing after another. God's grace is not limited. Moses gave us the Law.[2] Jesus Christ has given us grace and truth.

No one has ever seen God. But God, the one and only Son, is at the Father's side. He has shown us what God is like.

Many people have attempted to write about the things that have taken place among us. Reports of these things were handed down to us. There were people who saw these things for themselves from the beginning and then passed the word on.

I myself[3] have carefully looked into everything from the beginning. So it seemed good also to me to write down an orderly report of exactly what happened. I am doing this for you, most excellent Theophilus. I want you to know that the things you have been taught are true.

Herod was king of Judea.[4] During the time he was ruling, there was a priest named Zechariah. He belonged to a group of priests named after Abijah. His wife Elizabeth also came from the family line of Aaron. Both of them did what was right in God's eyes. They obeyed all the Lord's commandments and rules faithfully. But they had no children, because Elizabeth was not able to have any. And they were both very old.

One day Zechariah's group was on duty. He was serving as a priest in God's temple.[5] He happened to be chosen, in the usual way, to go into the temple of the Lord. There he was supposed to burn incense. The time came for this to be done. All who had gathered to worship were praying outside.

Then an angel of the Lord appeared to Zechariah. The angel was standing at the right side of the incense altar. When Zechariah saw him, he was amazed and terrified.

But the angel said to him, "Do not be afraid, Zechariah. Your prayer has been heard. Your wife Elizabeth will have a child. It will be a boy, and you must name him John. He will be a joy and delight to you. His birth will make many people very glad. He will be important in the Lord's eyes.

"He must never use wine or other such drinks. He will be filled with the Holy Spirit from the time he is born. He will bring many of Israel's people back to the Lord their God. And he will prepare the way for the Lord. He will have the same spirit and power that Elijah had.[6] He will teach parents how to love their children. He will also teach people who don't obey to be wise and do what is right. In this way, he will prepare a people who are ready for the Lord."

Zechariah asked the angel, "How can I be sure of this? I am an old man, and my wife is old too."

The angel answered, "I am Gabriel. I serve God. I have been sent to speak to you and to tell you this good news. And now you will have to be silent. You will not be able to speak until after John is born. That's because you did not believe my words. They will come true when the time is right."

During that time, the people were waiting for Zechariah to come out. They wondered why he stayed in the temple so long. When he came out, he could not speak to them. They realized he had seen a vision in the temple. They knew this because he kept motioning to them. He still could not speak.

When his time of service was over, he returned home. After that, his wife Elizabeth became pregnant. She stayed at home for five months. "The Lord has done this for me," she said. "In these days, he has been kind to me. He has taken away my shame among the people."

In the sixth month after Elizabeth had become pregnant, God sent the angel Gabriel to Nazareth, a town in Galilee. He was sent to a virgin. The girl was engaged to a man named Joseph. He came from the family line of David.[7] The virgin's name was Mary. The angel greeted her and said, "The Lord has given you special favor. He is with you."

Mary was very upset because of his words. She wondered what kind of greeting this could be. But the angel said to her, "Do not be afraid, Mary. God is very pleased with you. You will become pregnant and give birth to a son. You must name him Jesus.[8] He will be great and will be called the Son of the Most High God. The Lord God will make him a king like his father David of long ago. He will rule forever over his people, who came from Jacob's family. His kingdom will never end."

"How can this happen?" Mary asked the angel. "I am a virgin."

The angel answered, "The Holy Spirit will come to you. The power of the Most High God will cover you. So the holy one that is born will be called the Son of God. Your relative Elizabeth is old. And even she is going to have a child. People thought she could not have children. But she has been pregnant for six months now. Nothing is impossible with God."

"I serve the Lord," Mary answered. "May it happen to me just as you said it would." Then the angel left her.

At that time Mary got ready and hurried to a town in Judea's hill country. There she entered Zechariah's home and greeted Elizabeth. When Elizabeth heard Mary's greeting, the baby inside her jumped. And Elizabeth was filled with the Holy Spirit. In a loud voice she called out, "God has blessed you more than other women. And blessed is the child you will have! But why is God so kind to me? Why has the mother of my Lord come to me? As soon as I heard the sound of your voice, the baby inside me jumped for joy. You are a woman God has blessed. You have believed that what the Lord has said to you will be done!"

Mary said,

"My soul gives glory to the Lord.

My spirit delights in God my Savior.

He has taken note of me

even though I am not important.

From now on all people will call me blessed.

The Mighty One has done great things for me.

His name is holy.

He shows his mercy to those who have respect for him,
from parent to child down through the years.
He has done mighty things with his arm.
He has scattered those who are proud in their
deepest thoughts.
He has brought down rulers from their thrones.
But he has lifted up people who are not important.
He has filled those who are hungry with good things.
But he has sent those who are rich away empty.
He has helped the people of Israel, who serve him.
He has always remembered to be kind
to Abraham and his children down through the years.[9]
He has done it just as he said to our people of
long ago."

Mary stayed with Elizabeth about three months. Then she returned home.

The time came for Elizabeth to have her baby. She gave birth to a son. Her neighbors and relatives heard that the Lord had been very kind to her. They shared her joy.

On the eighth day, they came to have the child circumcised. They were going to name him Zechariah, like his father. But his mother spoke up. "No!" she said. "He must be called John."

They said to her, "No one among your relatives has that name."

Then they motioned to his father. They wanted to find out what he would like to name the child. He asked for something to write on. Then he wrote, "His name is John." Everyone was amazed.

Right away Zechariah could speak again. His first words gave praise to God. The neighbors were all filled with fear and wonder. All through Judea's hill country, people were talking about all these things. Everyone who heard this wondered about it. And because the Lord was with John, they asked, "What is this child going to be?"

His father Zechariah was filled with the Holy Spirit. He prophesied,

"Give praise to the Lord, the God of Israel!

He has come and set his people free.

He has acted with great power and has saved us.

He did it for those who are from the family line
of his servant David.

Long ago holy prophets said he would do it.

He has saved us from our enemies.

We are rescued from all who hate us.

He has been kind to our people.

He has remembered his holy covenant.

He made an oath to our father Abraham.

He promised to save us from our enemies,
so that we could serve him without fear.

He wants us to be holy and godly as long as we live.

"And you, my child, will be called a prophet of the
Most High God.

You will go ahead of the Lord to prepare the way
for him.

You will tell his people how they can be saved.

You will tell them that their sins can be forgiven.

All of that will happen because our God is tender
and caring.

His kindness will bring the rising sun to us from
heaven.

It will shine on those living in darkness
and in the shadow of death.

It will guide our feet on the path of peace."

The child grew up, and his spirit became strong. He lived in the desert until he appeared openly to Israel.

chapter two

A Special Birth

This is how the birth of Jesus Christ came about. His mother Mary and Joseph had promised to get married. But before they started to live together, it became clear that she was going to have a baby. She became pregnant by the power of the Holy Spirit. Her husband Joseph was a godly man. He did not want to put her to shame in public. So he planned to divorce her quietly.

But as Joseph was thinking about this, an angel of the Lord appeared to him in a dream. The angel said, "Joseph, son of David, don't be afraid to take Mary home as your wife. The baby inside her is from the Holy Spirit. She is going to have a son. You must give him the name Jesus. That is because he will save his people from their sins."

All of this took place to bring about what the Lord had said would happen. He had said through the prophet, "The virgin is going to have a baby. She will give birth to a son. And he will be called Immanuel."[1] The name Immanuel means "God with us."

Joseph woke up. He did what the angel of the Lord commanded him to do. He took Mary home as his wife. But he did not make love to her until after she gave birth to a son. And Joseph gave him the name Jesus.

Jesus was born in Bethlehem in Judea. This happened while Herod was king of Judea.

In those days, Caesar Augustus made a law. It required that a list be made of everyone in the whole Roman world. It was the first time a list was made of the people while Quirinius was governor of Syria. All went to their own towns to be listed.

So Joseph went also. He went from the town of Nazareth in Galilee to Judea. That is where Bethlehem, the town of David, was. Joseph went there because he belonged to the family line of David. He went there with Mary to be listed. Mary was engaged to him. She was expecting a baby.

While Joseph and Mary were there, the time came for the child to be born. She gave birth to her first baby. It was a boy. She wrapped him in large strips of cloth. Then she placed him in a manger.[2] There was no room for them in the inn.

There were shepherds living out in the fields nearby. It was night, and they were looking after their sheep. An angel of the Lord appeared to them. And the glory of the Lord shone around them. They were terrified.

But the angel said to them, "Do not be afraid. I bring you good news of great joy. It is for all the people. Today in the town of David a Savior has been born to you. He is Christ the Lord. Here is how you will know I am telling you the truth. You will find a baby wrapped in strips of cloth and lying in a manger."

Suddenly a large group of angels from heaven also appeared. They were praising God. They said,

"May glory be given to God in the highest heaven!

And may peace be given to those he is pleased

with on earth!"

The angels left and went into heaven. Then the shepherds said to one another, "Let's go to Bethlehem. Let's see this thing that has happened, which the Lord has told us about."

So they hurried off and found Mary and Joseph and the baby. The baby was lying in the manger. After the shepherds had seen him, they told everyone. They reported what the angel had said about this child. All who heard it were amazed at what the shepherds said to them.

But Mary kept all these things like a secret treasure in her heart. She thought about them over and over.

The shepherds returned. They gave glory and praise to God. Everything they had seen and heard was just as they had been told.

This is a record of the family line of Jesus Christ. He is the son of David. He is also the son of Abraham. [3] It was thought that he was the son of Joseph. Joseph was the husband of Mary. And Mary gave birth to Jesus, who is called Christ.

When the child was eight days old, he was circumcised. At the same time he was named Jesus. This was the name the angel had given him before his mother became pregnant.

The time for making them pure came as it is written in the Law of Moses. So Joseph and Mary took Jesus to Jerusalem. There they presented him to the Lord. In the Law of the Lord it says, "The first boy born in every family must be set apart for the Lord."[4] They also offered a sacrifice. They did it in keeping with the Law, which says, "a pair of doves or two young pigeons."[5]

In Jerusalem there was a man named Simeon. He was a good and godly man. He was waiting for God's promise to Israel to happen. The Holy Spirit was with him. The Spirit had told Simeon that he would not die before he had seen the Lord's Christ. The Spirit led him into the temple courtyard.

Then Jesus' parents brought the child in. They came to do for him what the Law required.

Simeon took Jesus in his arms and praised God. He said,

"Lord, you are the King over all.

Now let me, your servant, go in peace.

That is what you promised.

My eyes have seen your salvation.

You have prepared it in the sight of all people.

It is a light to be given to those who aren't Jews.

It will bring glory to your people Israel."

The child's father and mother were amazed at what was said about him. Then Simeon blessed them. He said to Mary, Jesus' mother, "This child is going to cause many people in Israel to fall and to rise. God has sent him. But many will speak against him. The thoughts of many hearts will be known. A sword will wound your own soul too."

There was also a prophet named Anna. She was the daughter of Penuel from the tribe of Asher. Anna was very old. After getting married, she lived with her husband seven years. Then she was a widow until she was 84. She never left the temple. She worshiped night and day, praying and going without eating.

Anna came up to Jesus' family at that very moment. She gave thanks to God. And she spoke about the child to all who were looking forward to the time when Jerusalem would be set free.

Joseph and Mary did everything the Law of the Lord required.

After Jesus' birth, Wise Men from the east came to Jerusalem. They asked, "Where is the child who has been born to be king of the Jews? When we were in the east, we saw his star. Now we have come to worship him."

When King Herod heard about it, he was very upset. Everyone in Jerusalem was troubled too. So Herod called together all the chief priests of the people. He also called the teachers of the law. He asked them where the Christ was going to be born.

"In Bethlehem in Judea," they replied. "This is what the prophet has written. He said,

"'But you, Bethlehem, in the land of Judah,

are certainly not the least important among the

towns of Judah.

A ruler will come out of you.

He will be the shepherd of my people Israel.'"[6]

Then Herod called for the Wise Men secretly. He found out from them exactly when the star had appeared. He sent them to Bethlehem. He said, "Go! Make a careful search for the child. As soon as you find him, bring me a report. Then I can go and worship him too."

After the Wise Men had listened to the king, they went on their way. The star they had seen when they were in the east went ahead of them. It finally stopped over the place where the child was. When they saw the star, they were filled with joy.

The Wise Men went to the house. There they saw the child with his mother Mary. They bowed down and worshiped him. Then they opened their treasures. They gave him gold, incense and myrrh.

But God warned them in a dream not to go back to Herod. So they returned to their country on a different road.

When the Wise Men had left, Joseph had a dream. In the dream an angel of the Lord appeared to him. "Get up!" the angel said. "Take the child and his mother and escape to Egypt. Stay there until I tell you to come back. Herod is going to search for the child. He wants to kill him."

Joseph got up. During the night, he left for Egypt with the child and his mother Mary. They stayed there until King Herod died. So the words the Lord had spoken through the prophet came true. He had said, "I chose to bring my son out of Egypt."[7]

Herod realized that the Wise Men had tricked him. So he became very angry. He gave orders concerning Bethlehem and the area around it. All the boys two years old and under were to be killed. This agreed with the time when the Wise Men had seen the star.

In this way, the words the prophet Jeremiah spoke came true. He had said,

"A voice is heard in Ramah.

It's the sound of crying and deep sadness.

Rachel is crying over her children.

She refuses to be comforted,

because they are gone."[8]

After Herod died,[9] Joseph had a dream while he was still in Egypt. In the dream an angel of the Lord appeared to him. The angel said, "Get up! Take the child and his mother. Go to the land of Israel. Those who were trying to kill the child are dead."

So Joseph got up. He took the child and his mother Mary back to the land of Israel. But then he heard that Archelaus was king of Judea. Archelaus was ruling in place of his father Herod. This made Joseph afraid to go there.

Warned in a dream, Joseph went back to the land of Galilee instead. There he lived in a town called Nazareth. So what the prophets had said about Jesus came true. They had said, "He will be called a Nazarene."

And the child grew and became strong. He was very wise. He was blessed by God's grace.

Every year Jesus' parents went to Jerusalem for the Passover Feast.[10] When he was 12 years old, they went up to the Feast as usual.

After the Feast was over, his parents left to go back home. The boy Jesus stayed behind in Jerusalem. But they were not aware of it. They thought he was somewhere in their group. So they traveled on for a day.

Then they began to look for him among their relatives and friends. They did not find him. So they went back to Jerusalem to look for him. After three days they found him in the temple court-yard. He was sitting with the teachers. He was listening to them and asking them questions. Everyone who heard him was amazed at how much he understood. They also were amazed at his answers.

When his parents saw him, they were amazed. His mother said to him, "Son, why have you treated us like this? Your father and I have been worried about you. We have been looking for you every-where."

"Why were you looking for me?" he asked. "Didn't you know I had to be in my Father's house?" But they did not understand what he meant by that.

Then he went back to Nazareth with them, and he obeyed them. But his mother kept all these things like a secret treasure in her heart. Jesus became wiser and stronger. He also became more and more pleasing to God and to people.

chapter three

Preparing the Way

A man came who was sent from God. His name was John.[1] He came to give witness about that light. He gave witness so that all people could believe. John himself was not the light. He came only as a witness to the light.

John gives witness about him. He cries out and says, "This was the one I was talking about. I said, 'He who comes after me is more important than I am. He is more important because he existed before I was born.'"

Tiberius Caesar had been ruling for 15 years. Pontius Pilate was governor of Judea. Herod was the ruler of Galilee. His brother Philip was the ruler of Iturea and Traconitis. Lysanias was ruler of Abilene.[2] Annas and Caiaphas were high priests.

At that time God's word came to John, son of Zechariah, in the desert. He went into all the countryside around the Jordan River. There he preached that people should be baptized and turn away from their sins.[3] Then God would forgive them. He said, "Turn away from your sins! The kingdom of heaven is near."

John is the one the prophet Isaiah had spoken about. Long ago Isaiah the prophet wrote,

"I will send my messenger ahead of you.

He will prepare your way."[4]

"A messenger is calling out in the desert,

'Prepare the way for the Lord.

Make straight paths for him.

Every valley will be filled in.

Every mountain and hill will be made level.

The crooked roads will become straight.

The rough ways will become smooth.

And everyone will see God's salvation.'"[5]

And so John came. He baptized people in the desert. All the people from the countryside of Judea went out to him. All the people from Jerusalem went too. When they admitted they had sinned, John baptized them in the Jordan River.

John wore clothes made out of camel's hair. He had a leather belt around his waist. And he ate locusts and wild honey.

John saw many Pharisees and Sadducees[6] coming to where he was baptizing. He said, "You are like a nest of poisonous snakes! Who warned you to escape the coming of God's anger? Produce fruit that shows you have turned away from your sins. And don't start saying to yourselves, 'Abraham is our father.' I tell you, God can raise up children for Abraham even from these stones. The ax is already lying at the roots of the trees. All the trees that don't produce good fruit will be cut down. They will be thrown into the fire."

"Then what should we do?" the crowd asked.

John answered, "If you have extra clothes, you should share with those who have none. And if you have extra food, you should do the same."

Tax collectors also came to be baptized. "Teacher," they asked, "what should we do?"

"Don't collect any more than you are required to," John told them.

Then some soldiers asked him, "And what should we do?"

John replied, "Don't force people to give you money. Don't bring false charges against people. Be happy with your pay."

The people were waiting. They were expecting something. They were all wondering in their hearts if John might be the Christ.[7]

John answered them all, "I baptize you with water. But One who is more powerful than I will come. I'm not good enough to untie the straps of his sandals. He will baptize you with the Holy Spirit and with fire. His pitchfork is in his hand to toss the straw away from his threshing floor. He will gather his wheat into the storeroom. But he will burn up the husks with fire that can't be put out."

John said many other things to warn the people. He also preached the good news to them.

Jesus was about 30 years old when he began his special work for God and others. Jesus came from Galilee to the Jordan River. He wanted to be baptized by John. But John tried to stop him. He told Jesus, "I need to be baptized by you. So why do you come to me?"

Jesus replied, "Let it be this way for now. It is right for us to do this. It carries out God's holy plan."

Then John agreed. When all the people were being baptized, Jesus was baptized too. John baptized him in the Jordan River.

Jesus was coming up out of the water. Just then, he saw heaven being torn open. He saw the Holy Spirit coming down on him like a dove.

A voice spoke to him from heaven. It said, "You are my Son, and I love you. I am very pleased with you."

Jesus, full of the Holy Spirit, returned from the Jordan River. The Spirit led him into the desert. There the devil tempted him for 40 days.

Jesus ate nothing during that time. After 40 days and 40 nights of going without eating, Jesus was hungry.

The tempter came to him. He said, "If you are the Son of God, tell these stones to become bread."

Jesus answered, "It is written, 'Man doesn't live only on bread.

He also lives on every word that comes from the mouth of God.'"[8]

Then the devil took Jesus to the holy city. He had him stand on the highest point of the temple. "If you are the Son of God," he said, "throw yourself down. It is written,

"'The Lord will command his angels to take good

care of you.

They will lift you up in their hands.

Then you won't trip over a stone.'"[9]

Jesus answered him, "It is also written, 'Do not put the Lord your God to the test.'"[10]

Finally, the devil took Jesus to a very high mountain. He showed him all the kingdoms of the world and their glory. He said to him, "I will give you all their authority and glory. It has been given to me, and I can give it to anyone I want to. If you bow down and worship me," he said, "I will give you all of this."

Jesus said to him, "Get away from me, Satan! It is written, 'Worship the Lord your God. He is the only one you should serve.'"[11]

When the devil finished all this tempting, he left Jesus until a better time. The wild animals didn't harm Jesus. Angels came and took care of him.

The Jews of Jerusalem sent priests and Levites to ask John who he was. John gave witness to them. He did not try to hide the truth. He spoke to them openly. He said, "I am not the Christ."

They asked him, "Then who are you? Are you Elijah?"[12]

He said, "I am not."

"Are you the Prophet we've been expecting?" they asked.

"No," he answered.

They asked one last time, "Who are you? Give us an answer to take back to those who sent us. What do you say about yourself?"

John replied, using the words of Isaiah the prophet. John said,

"I'm the messenger who is calling out in the desert, 'Make the way for the Lord straight.'"[13]

Some Pharisees who had been sent asked him, "If you are not the Christ, why are you baptizing people? Why are you doing that if you aren't Elijah or the Prophet we've been expecting?"

"I baptize people with water," John replied. "But One is standing among you whom you do not know. He is the One who comes after me. I am not good enough to untie his sandals."

This all happened at Bethany on the other side of the Jordan River. That was where John was baptizing.

The next day John saw Jesus coming toward him. John said, "Look! The Lamb of God! He takes away the sin of the world![14] This is the One I was talking about. I said, 'A man who comes after me is more important than I am. That's because he existed before I was born.' I did not know him. But God wants to make it clear to Israel who this person is. That's the reason I came baptizing with water."

Then John told them, "I saw the Holy Spirit come down from heaven like a dove. The Spirit remained on Jesus. I would not have known him. But the One who sent me to baptize with water told me, 'You will see the Spirit come down and remain on someone. He is the One who will baptize with the Holy Spirit.' I have seen it happen. I give witness that this is the Son of God."

chapter four

Jesus Starts His Mission

The next day John was again with two of his disciples. He saw Jesus walking by. John said, "Look! The Lamb of God!"

The two disciples heard him say this. So they followed Jesus.

Then Jesus turned around and saw them following. He asked, "What do you want?"

They said, "Rabbi, where are you staying?" Rabbi means Teacher.

"Come," he replied. "You will see."

So they went and saw where he was staying. They spent the rest of the day with him. It was about four o'clock in the afternoon.

Andrew was Simon Peter's brother. Andrew was one of the two disciples who heard what John had said. He had also followed Jesus. The first thing Andrew did was to find his brother Simon. He told him, "We have found the Messiah." Messiah means Christ. And he brought Simon to Jesus.

Jesus looked at him and said, "You are Simon, son of John. You will be called Cephas." Cephas means Peter (or rock).[1]

The next day Jesus decided to leave for Galilee. He found Philip and said to him, "Follow me."

Philip was from the town of Bethsaida. So were Andrew and Peter. Philip found Nathanael and told him, "We have found the One that Moses wrote about in the Law. The prophets also wrote about him. He is Jesus of Nazareth, the son of Joseph."

"Nazareth! Can anything good come from there?" Nathanael asked.

"Come and see," said Philip.

Jesus saw Nathanael approaching. Here is what Jesus said about him. "He is a true Israelite. There is nothing false in him."

"How do you know me?" Nathanael asked.

Jesus answered, "I saw you while you were still under the fig tree. I saw you there before Philip called you."

Nathanael replied, "Rabbi, you are the Son of God. You are the King of Israel."

Jesus said, "You believe because I told you I saw you under the fig tree. You will see greater things than that."

Then he said to the disciples, "What I'm about to tell you is true. You will see heaven open. You will see the angels of God going up and coming down on the Son of Man."

On the third day there was a wedding. It took place at Cana in Galilee. Jesus' mother was there. Jesus and his disciples had also been invited to the wedding. When the wine was gone, Jesus' mother said to him, "They have no more wine."

"Dear woman, why do you bring me into this?" Jesus replied. "My time has not yet come."

His mother said to the servants, "Do what he tells you."

Six stone water jars stood nearby. The Jews used water from that kind of jar for special washings to make themselves pure. Each jar could hold 20 to 30 gallons.

Jesus said to the servants, "Fill the jars with water." So they filled them to the top.

Then he told them, "Now dip some out. Take it to the person in charge of the dinner."

They did what he said. The person in charge tasted the water that had been turned into wine. He didn't realize where it had come from. But the servants who had brought the water knew.

Then the person in charge called the groom to one side. He said to him, "Everyone brings out the best wine first. They bring out the cheaper wine after the guests have had too much to drink. But you have saved the best until now."

That was the first of Jesus' miraculous signs. He did it at Cana in Galilee. Jesus showed his glory by doing it. And his disciples put their faith in him.

After this, Jesus went down to Capernaum. His mother and brothers and disciples went with him. They all stayed there for a few days.

It was almost time for the Jewish Passover Feast. So Jesus went up to Jerusalem. In the temple courtyard he found people who were selling cattle, sheep and doves. Others were sitting at tables exchanging money.[2]

So Jesus made a whip out of ropes. He chased all the sheep and cattle from the temple area. He scattered the coins of the people exchanging money. And he turned over their tables. He told those who were selling doves, "Get these out of here! How dare you turn my Father's house into a market!"

His disciples remembered what had been written. It says, "My great love for your house will destroy me."[3]

Then the Jews asked him, "What miraculous sign can you show us? Can you prove your authority to do all of this?"

Jesus answered them, "Destroy this temple. I will raise it up again in three days."

The Jews replied, "It has taken 46 years to build this temple. Are you going to raise it up in three days?"

But the temple Jesus had spoken about was his body.

His disciples later remembered what he had said. That was

after he had been raised from the dead. Then they believed the Scriptures. They also believed the words that Jesus had spoken.

Meanwhile, he was in Jerusalem at the Passover Feast. Many people saw the miraculous signs he was doing. And they believed in his name. But Jesus did not fully trust them. He knew what people are like. He didn't need others to tell him what people are like. He already knew what was in the human heart.

There was a Pharisee named Nicodemus. He was one of the Jewish rulers. He came to Jesus at night and said, "Rabbi, we know you are a teacher who has come from God. We know that God is with you. If he weren't, you couldn't do the miraculous signs you are doing."

Jesus replied, "What I'm about to tell you is true. No one can see God's kingdom without being born again."

"How can I be born when I am old?" Nicodemus asked. "I can't go back inside my mother! I can't be born a second time!"

Jesus answered, "What I'm about to tell you is true. No one can enter God's kingdom without being born through water and the Holy Spirit. People give birth to people. But the Spirit gives birth to spirit. You should not be surprised when I say, 'You must all be born again.'

"The wind blows where it wants to. You hear the sound it makes. But you can't tell where it comes from or where it is going. It is the same with everyone who is born through the Spirit."

"How can this be?" Nicodemus asked.

"You are Israel's teacher," said Jesus. "Don't you understand these things?

"What I'm about to tell you is true. We speak about what we know. We give witness to what we have seen. But still you people do not accept our witness. I have spoken to you about earthly things, and you do not believe. So how will you believe if I speak about heavenly things?

"No one has ever gone into heaven except the One who came from heaven. He is the Son of Man. Moses lifted up the snake in the desert. [4] The Son of Man must be lifted up also. Then everyone who believes in him can live with God forever.

"God loved the world so much that he gave his one and only Son. Anyone who believes in him will not die but will have eternal life.

"God did not send his Son into the world to judge the world. He sent his Son to save the world through him. Anyone who believes in him is not judged. But anyone who does not believe is judged already. He has not believed in the name of God's one and only Son.

"Here is the judgment. Light has come into the world, but people loved darkness instead of light. They loved darkness because what they did was evil.

"Everyone who does evil things hates the light. They will not come into the light. They are afraid that what they do will be seen. But anyone who lives by the truth comes into the light. He does this so that it will be easy to see that what he has done is with God's help."

After this, Jesus and his disciples went out into the countryside of Judea. There he spent some time with them. And he baptized people there.

John was also baptizing. He was at Aenon near Salim, where there was plenty of water. People were coming all the time to be baptized. That was before John was put in prison.

Some of John's disciples and a certain Jew began to argue. They argued about special washings to make people "clean." They came to John and said to him, "Rabbi, that man who was with you on the other side of the Jordan River is baptizing people. He is the one you gave witness about. Everyone is going to him."

John replied, "A person can receive only what God gives him from heaven. You yourselves are witnesses that I said, 'I am not the Christ. I was sent ahead of him.' The bride belongs to the groom. The friend who helps the groom waits and listens for him. He is full of joy when he hears the groom's voice. That joy is mine, and it is now complete. He must become more important. I must become less important.

"The One who comes from above is above everything. The one who is from the earth belongs to the earth and speaks like someone from the earth. The One who comes from heaven is above everything. He gives witness to what he has seen and heard. But no one accepts what he says. Anyone who has accepted it has said, 'Yes. God is truthful.' The One whom God has sent speaks God's words. God gives the Holy Spirit without limit.

"The Father loves the Son and has put everything into his hands. Anyone who believes in the Son has eternal life. Anyone who says no to the Son will not have life. God's anger remains on him."

The Pharisees heard that Jesus was winning and baptizing more disciples than John. But in fact Jesus was not baptizing. His disciples were.

But John found fault with Herod, the ruler of Galilee, because of Herodias. She was the wife of Herod's brother. John also spoke strongly to Herod about all the other evil things he had done. So Herod locked him up in prison. He added this sin to all his others.

After John was put in prison, Jesus went into Galilee. He had to go through Samaria. He came to a town in Samaria called Sychar. It was near the piece of land Jacob had given his son Joseph. Jacob's well was there. Jesus was tired from the journey. So he sat down by the well. It was about noon.

A woman from Samaria came to get some water. Jesus said to her, "Will you give me a drink?" His disciples had gone into the town to buy food.

The Samaritan woman said to him, "You are a Jew. I am a Samaritan woman. How can you ask me for a drink?" She said this because Jews don't have anything to do with Samaritans.[5]

Jesus answered her, "You do not know what God's gift is. And you do not know who is asking you for a drink. If you did, you would have asked him. He would have given you living water."

"Sir," the woman said, "you don't have anything to get water with. The well is deep. Where can you get this living water?

"Our father Jacob gave us the well. He drank from it himself. So did his sons and his flocks and herds. Are you more important than he is?"

Jesus answered, "All who drink this water will be thirsty again. But anyone who drinks the water I give him will never be thirsty. In fact, the water I give him will become a spring of water in him. It will flow up into eternal life."

The woman said to him, "Sir, give me this water. Then I will never be thirsty. And I won't have to keep coming here to get water."

He told her, "Go. Get your husband and come back."

"I have no husband," she replied.

Jesus said to her, "You are right when you say you have no husband. The fact is, you have had five husbands. And the man you have now is not your husband. What you have just said is very true."

"Sir," the woman said, "I can see that you are a prophet. Our people have worshiped on this mountain for a long time. But you Jews claim that the place where we must worship is in Jerusalem."

Jesus said, "Believe me, woman. A time is coming when you will not worship the Father on this mountain or in Jerusalem. You Samaritans worship what you do not know. We worship what we do know. Salvation comes from the Jews.

"But a new time is coming. In fact, it is already here. True worshipers will worship the Father in spirit and in truth. They are the kind of worshipers the Father is looking for.

"God is spirit. His worshipers must worship him in spirit and in truth."

The woman said, "I know that Messiah is coming." (He is called Christ.) "When he comes, he will explain everything to us."

Then Jesus said, "I, the one speaking to you, am he."

Just then Jesus' disciples returned. They were surprised to find him talking with a woman.[6] But no one asked, "What do you want from her?" No one asked, "Why are you talking with her?"

The woman left her water jar and went back to the town. She said to the people, "Come. See a man who told me everything I've ever done. Could this be the Christ?"

The people came out of the town and made their way toward Jesus.

His disciples were saying to him, "Rabbi, eat something!"

But he said to them, "I have food to eat that you know nothing about."

Then his disciples asked each other, "Did someone bring him food?"

Jesus said, "My food is to do what my Father sent me to do. My food is to finish his work.

"You say, 'Four months more, and then it will be harvest time.' But I tell you, open your eyes! Look at the fields! They are ripe for harvest right now. Those who gather the crop are already getting paid. They are already harvesting the crop for eternal life. So those who plant and those who gather can now be glad together.

"Here is a true saying. 'One plants and another gathers.' I sent you to gather what you have not worked for. Others have done the hard work. You have gathered the benefits of their work."

Many of the Samaritans from the town of Sychar believed in Jesus. They believed because of the woman's witness. She said, "He told me everything I've ever done."

Then the Samaritans came to him and tried to get him to stay with them. So he stayed two days. Because of his words, many more people became believers.

They said to the woman, "We no longer believe just because of what you said. We have now heard for ourselves. We know that this man really is the Savior of the world."

After the two days, Jesus left for Galilee.

When he arrived in Galilee, the people living there welcomed him.

They had seen everything he had done in Jerusalem at the Passover Feast. That was because they had also been there.

Once more, Jesus visited Cana in Galilee. Cana is where he had turned the water into wine. A royal official was there. His son was sick in bed at Capernaum. The official heard that Jesus had arrived in Galilee from Judea. So he went to Jesus and begged him to come and heal his son. The boy was close to death.

Jesus told him, "You people will never believe unless you see miraculous signs and wonders."

The royal official said, "Sir, come down before my child dies."

Jesus replied, "You may go. Your son will live."

The man believed what Jesus said, and so he left. While he was still on his way home, his servants met him. They gave him the news that his boy was living. He asked what time his son got better. They said to him, "The fever left him yesterday afternoon at one o'clock."

Then the father realized what had happened. That was the exact time Jesus had said to him, "Your son will live." So he and all his family became believers.

This was the second miraculous sign that Jesus did after coming from Judea to Galilee.

chapter five

Opposition Begins

J esus went to Nazareth, where he had been brought up. On the Sabbath day he went into the synagogue as he usually did. And he stood up to read.

The scroll of the prophet Isaiah was handed to him. He unrolled it and found the right place. There it is written,

"The Spirit of the Lord is on me.

He has anointed me

to tell the good news to poor people.

He has sent me to announce freedom for prisoners.

He has sent me so that the blind will see again.

He wants me to free those who are beaten down.

And he has sent me to announce the year when

he will set his people free."[1]

Then Jesus rolled up the scroll. He gave it back to the attendant and sat down. The eyes of everyone in the synagogue were staring at him.

He began by saying to them, "Today this passage of Scripture is coming true as you listen."

Everyone said good things about him. They were amazed at the gracious words they heard from his lips. "Isn't this Joseph's son?" they asked.

Jesus said, "Here is a saying you will certainly apply to me. 'Doctor, heal yourself! Do the things here in your hometown that we heard you did in Capernaum.'"

"What I'm about to tell you is true," he continued. "A prophet is not accepted in his hometown. I tell you for sure that there were many widows in Israel in the days of Elijah. And there had been no rain for three and a half years. There wasn't enough food to eat anywhere in the land. But Elijah was not sent to any of those widows. Instead, he was sent to a widow in Zarephath near Sidon. And there were many in Israel who had skin diseases in the days of Elisha the prophet. But not one of them was healed except Naaman the Syrian."[2]

All the people in the synagogue were very angry when they heard that. They got up and ran Jesus out of town. They took him to the edge of the hill on which the town was built. They planned to throw him down the cliff. But Jesus walked right through the crowd and went on his way.

Jesus left Nazareth. He went to live in the city of Capernaum. It was by the lake in the area of Zebulun and Naphtali.[3] In that way, what the prophet Isaiah had said came true. He had said,

"Land of Zebulun! Land of Naphtali!

Galilee, where non-Jewish people live!

Land along the Mediterranean Sea! Territory east

of the Jordan River!

The people who are now living in darkness

will see a great light.

They are now living in a very dark land.

But a light will shine on them."[4]

From that time on Jesus began to preach. "Turn away from your sins!" he said. "The kingdom of heaven is near. Turn away from your sins and believe the good news!"

One day Jesus was standing by the Sea of Galilee. The people crowded around him and listened to the word of God. Jesus saw two boats at the edge of the water. They had been left there by the fishermen, who were washing their nets. He got into the boat that belonged to Simon. Jesus asked him to go out a little way from shore. Then he sat down in the boat and taught the people.

When he finished speaking, he turned to Simon. He said, "Go out into deep water. Let the nets down so you can catch some fish."

Simon answered, "Master, we've worked hard all night and haven't caught anything. But because you say so, I will let down the nets."

When they had done so, they caught a large number of fish. There were so many that their nets began to break. So they motioned to their partners in the other boat to come and help them. They came and filled both boats so full that they began to sink.

When Simon Peter saw this, he fell at Jesus' knees. "Go away from me, Lord!" he said. "I am a sinful man!"

He and everyone with him were amazed at the number of fish they had caught. So were James and John, the sons of Zebedee, who worked with Simon.

Then Jesus said to Simon, "Don't be afraid. From now on you will catch people. Come. Follow me," Jesus said, "I will make you fishers of people."

At once they left their nets and followed him.

Going on from there, he saw two other brothers. They were James, son of Zebedee, and his brother John. They were in a boat with their father Zebedee. As they were preparing their nets, Jesus called out to them. Right away they left the boat and their father and followed Jesus.

Jesus and those with him went to Capernaum. When the Sabbath day came, he went into the synagogue. There he began to teach. The people were amazed at his teaching. He taught them like one who had authority. He did not talk like the teachers of the law.

In the synagogue there was a man controlled by a demon, an evil spirit. [5] He cried out at the top of his voice. "Ha!" he said. "What do you want with us, Jesus of Nazareth? Have you come to destroy us? I know who you are. You are the Holy One of God!"

"Be quiet!" Jesus said firmly. "Come out of him!"

The evil spirit shook the man wildly. Then the demon threw the man down in front of everybody. And it came out without hurting him.

All the people were amazed. They said to each other, "What is this teaching? With authority and power he gives orders to evil spirits. And they come out!"

The news about Jesus spread throughout the whole area.

Jesus and those with him left the synagogue. Right away they went with James and John to the house of Simon and Andrew. Simon's mother-in-law was lying in bed. She had a fever. They told Jesus about her. So he went to her. He bent over her and commanded the fever to leave, and it left her. He took her hand and helped her up. She got up at once and began to serve them.

That evening after sunset, the people brought to Jesus all who were sick. They also brought all who were controlled by demons. All the people in town gathered at the door.

Jesus healed many of them. They had all kinds of sicknesses. He placed his hands on each one and healed them.

He also drove out many demons. He drove out the spirits with a word. The demons shouted, "You are the Son of God!" But he commanded them to be quiet. He would not allow them to speak, because they knew he was the Christ.

He did it to make what the prophet Isaiah had said come true. He had said,

"He suffered the things we should have suffered.

He took on himself the sicknesses that should

have been ours."[6]

It was very early in the morning and still dark. Jesus got up and left the house. He went to a place where he could be alone. There he prayed. Simon and his friends went to look for Jesus. When they found him, they called out, "Everyone is looking for you!"

Jesus replied, "Let's go somewhere else. I want to go to the nearby towns. I must preach there also. That is why I have come."

So he traveled all around Galilee. There he taught in the synagogues. He preached the good news of God's kingdom. He healed every illness and sickness the people had.

News about him spread all over Syria. People brought to him all who were ill with different kinds of sicknesses. Some were suffering great pain. Others were controlled by demons. Some were shaking wildly. Others couldn't move at all. And Jesus healed all of them.

Large crowds followed him. Some people came from Galilee, from the area known as the Ten Cities, and from Jerusalem and Judea. Others came from the area across the Jordan River.

While Jesus was in one of the towns, a man came along. He had a skin disease all over his body. When he saw Jesus, he fell with his face to the ground. He begged him, "Lord, if you are willing to make me 'clean,' you can do it."

Jesus was filled with deep concern. He reached out his hand and touched the man. "I am willing to do it," he said. "Be 'clean'!" Right away the disease left him. He was healed.

Jesus sent him away at once. He gave the man a strong warning. "Don't tell this to anyone," he said. "Go and show yourself to the priest. Offer the sacrifices that Moses commanded. It will be a witness to the priest and the people that you are 'clean.'"

But the man went out and started talking right away. He spread the news to everyone. So Jesus could no longer enter a town openly. He stayed outside in lonely places.

But the news about Jesus spread even more. So crowds of people came to hear him. They also came to be healed of their sicknesses. But Jesus often went away to be by himself and pray.

A few days later, Jesus entered Capernaum again. The people heard that he had come home. So many people gathered that there was no room left. There was not even room outside the door. And Jesus preached the word to them.

Pharisees and teachers of the law were sitting there. They had come from every village of Galilee and from Judea and Jerusalem. They heard that the Lord had given Jesus the power to heal the sick.

Some men came carrying a man who could not walk. He was lying on a mat. They tried to take him into the house to place him in front of Jesus. They could not find a way to do this because of the crowd. So they went up on the roof. They made a hole in the roof above Jesus. Then they lowered the man on his mat through the opening in the roof tiles. They lowered him into the middle of the crowd, right in front of Jesus.

When Jesus saw that they had faith, he said, "Friend, your sins are forgiven."

The Pharisees and the teachers of the law began to think, "Who is this fellow who says such an evil thing? Who can forgive sins but God alone?"

Jesus knew what they were thinking. So he asked, "Why are you thinking these things in your hearts? Is it easier to say, 'Your sins are forgiven'? Or to say, 'Get up and walk'? I want you to know that the Son of Man[7] has authority on earth to forgive sins."

So he spoke to the man who could not walk. "I tell you," he said, "get up. Take your mat and go home."

Right away, the man stood up in front of them. He took his mat and went home praising God.

When the crowd saw this, they were filled with wonder. All the people were amazed. They praised God and said, "We have never seen anything like this!"

As Jesus went on from there, he saw a man named Matthew.[8]

He was sitting at the tax collector's booth.

"Follow me," Jesus told him. Matthew got up and followed him.

Later Jesus was having dinner at Matthew's house. Many tax collectors and "sinners" came. They ate with Jesus and his disciples.

The Pharisees saw this. So they asked the disciples, "Why does your teacher eat with tax collectors and 'sinners'?"

Jesus heard that. So he said, "Those who are healthy don't need a doctor. Sick people do. Go and learn what this means, 'I want mercy and not sacrifice.'[9] I have not come to get those who think they are right with God to follow me. I have come to get sinners to turn away from their sins."

Some of the people who were there said to Jesus, "John's disciples often pray and go without eating. So do the disciples of the Pharisees. But yours go on eating and drinking."

Jesus answered, "How can the guests of the groom go without eating while he is with them? They will not fast as long as he is with them. But the time will come when the groom will be taken away from them. On that day they will go without eating."

Then Jesus gave them an example. He said, "People don't tear a patch from new clothes and sew it on old clothes. If they do, they will tear the new clothes. Also, the patch from the new clothes will not match the old clothes. People don't pour new wine into old wineskins. If they do, the new wine will burst the skins. The wine will run out, and the wineskins will be destroyed. No, new wine must be poured into new wineskins. Then both are saved. After people drink old wine, they don't want the new. They say, 'The old wine is better.'"

Some time later, Jesus went up to Jerusalem for a Jewish feast. In Jerusalem near the Sheep Gate is a pool. In the Aramaic language it is called Bethesda. It is surrounded by five rows of columns with a roof over them. Here a great number of disabled people used to lie down. Among them were those who were blind, those who could not walk and those who could hardly move.

One person who was there had been disabled for 38 years. Jesus saw him lying there. He knew that the man had been in that condition for a long time. So he asked him, "Do you want to get well?"

"Sir," the disabled man replied, "I have no one to help me into the pool when an angel stirs the water up. I try to get in, but someone else always goes down ahead of me."

Then Jesus said to him, "Get up! Pick up your mat and walk."

At once the man was healed. He picked up his mat and walked.

The day this happened was a Sabbath. So the Jews said to the man who had been healed, "It is the Sabbath. The law does not allow you to carry your mat."[10]

But he replied, "The one who made me well said to me, 'Pick up your mat and walk.'"

They asked him, "Who is this fellow? Who told you to pick it up and walk?"

The one who was healed had no idea who it was. Jesus had slipped away into the crowd that was there.

Later Jesus found him at the temple. Jesus said to him, "See, you are well again. Stop sinning, or something worse may happen to you." The man went away. He told the Jews it was Jesus who had made him well.

Jesus was doing these things on the Sabbath day. So the Jews began to oppose him.

Jesus said to them, "My Father is always doing his work. He is working right up to this very day. I am working too."

For this reason the Jews tried even harder to kill him. Jesus was not only breaking the Sabbath. He was even calling God his own Father. He was making himself equal with God.

Jesus answered, "What I'm about to tell you is true. The Son can do nothing by himself. He can do only what he sees his Father doing. What the Father does, the Son also does. This is because the Father loves the Son. He shows him everything he does. Yes, you will be amazed! The Father will show him even greater things than these.

"The Father raises the dead and gives them life. In the same way, the Son gives life to anyone he wants to.

"Also, the Father does not judge anyone. He has given the Son the task of judging. Then all people will honor the Son just as they honor the Father. Those who do not honor the Son do not honor the Father, who sent him.

"What I'm about to tell you is true. Anyone who hears my word and believes him who sent me has eternal life. He will not be found guilty. He has crossed over from death to life.

"What I'm about to tell you is true. A time is coming for me to give life. In fact, it has already begun. The dead will hear the voice of the Son of God. Those who hear it will live.

"The Father has life in himself. He has also allowed the Son to have life in himself. And the Father has given him the authority to judge. This is because he is the Son of Man.

"Do not be amazed at this. A time is coming when all who are in the grave will hear his voice. They will all come out of their graves. Those who have done good will rise and live again. Those who have done evil will rise and be found guilty.

"I can do nothing by myself. I judge only as I hear. And my judging is fair. I do not try to please myself. I try only to please the One who sent me.

"If I give witness about myself, it doesn't count. There is someone else who gives witness in my favor. And I know that his witness about me counts.

"You have sent people to John. He has given witness to the truth. I do not accept human witness. I only talk about it so you can be saved. John was like a lamp that burned and gave light. For a while you chose to enjoy his light.

"The witness I have is more important than John's. I am doing the very work the Father gave me to finish. It gives witness that the Father has sent me.

"The Father who sent me has himself given witness about me. You have never heard his voice. You have never seen what he really looks like. And his word does not live in you. This is because you do not believe the One he sent.

"You study the Scriptures carefully. You study them because you think they will give you eternal life. The Scriptures you study give witness about me. But you refuse to come to me and receive life.

"I do not accept praise from people. But I know you. I know that you do not have love for God in your hearts. I have come in my Father's name, and you do not accept me. But if someone else comes in his own name, you will accept him.

"You accept praise from one another. But you make no effort to receive the praise that comes from the only God. So how can you believe?

"Do not think I will bring charges against you in front of the Father. Moses is the one who does that. And he is the one you build your hopes on.

"Do you believe Moses? Then you should believe me. He wrote about me. But you do not believe what he wrote. So how are you going to believe what I say?"

One Sabbath day Jesus was walking with his disciples through the grain fields. His disciples were hungry. So they began to break off some heads of grain and eat them. The Pharisees saw this. They said to Jesus, "Look! It is against the Law to do this on the Sabbath. But your disciples are doing it anyway!"

Jesus answered, "Haven't you ever read about what David did? He and his men were hungry. He entered the house of God and took the holy bread. He ate the bread that only priests were allowed to eat. David also gave some to his men."[11]

Then Jesus said to them, "The Son of Man is Lord of the Sabbath Day. Haven't you read the Law? It tells how every Sabbath day the priests in the temple have to do their work on that day. But they are not considered guilty.

"I tell you that one who is more important than the temple is here. Scripture says, 'I want mercy and not sacrifice.'[12] You don't know what those words mean. If you did, you would not bring charges against those who are not guilty.

"The Sabbath day was made for man. Man was not made for the Sabbath day. So the Son of Man is Lord even of the Sabbath day."

On another Sabbath day, Jesus went into the synagogue and was teaching. A man whose right hand was weak and twisted was there. The Pharisees and the teachers of the law were trying to find fault with Jesus. So they watched him closely. They wanted to see if he would heal on the Sabbath.

But Jesus knew what they were thinking. He spoke to the man who had the weak and twisted hand. "Get up and stand in front of everyone," he said. So the man got up and stood there.

The Pharisees were trying to find fault with Jesus. So they asked him, "Does the Law allow us to heal on the Sabbath day?"

He said to them, "What if one of your sheep falls into a pit on the Sabbath? Won't you take hold of it and lift it out? A man is worth more than sheep! So the Law allows us to do good on the Sabbath day."

Then Jesus asked them, "What does the Law say we should do on the Sabbath day? Should we do good? Or should we do evil? Should we save life? Or should we kill?" But no one answered.

Jesus looked around at them in anger. He was very upset because their hearts were stubborn. Then he said to the man, "Stretch out your hand." He stretched it out, and his hand was as good as new.

But the Pharisees and the teachers of the law were very angry. They began to talk to each other about what they might do to Jesus. Then the Pharisees went out and began to make plans with the Herodians. They wanted to kill Jesus.

Jesus knew all about the Pharisees' plans. So he left that place. Many followed him, and he healed all their sick people.

chapter six

Teaching the People

J esus went off to the Sea of Galilee with his disciples. A large crowd from Galilee followed. People heard about all that Jesus was doing. And many came to him. They came from Judea, Jerusalem, and Idumea. They came from the lands east of the Jordan River. And they came from the area around Tyre and Sidon.

Because of the crowd, Jesus told his disciples to get a small boat ready for him. This would keep the people from crowding him. Jesus had healed many people. So those who were sick were pushing forward to touch him.

When people with evil spirits saw him, they fell down in front of him. The spirits shouted, "You are the Son of God!" But Jesus ordered them not to tell who he was. This was to make what was spoken through the prophet Isaiah come true. It says,

"Here is my servant. I have chosen him.

He is the one I love. I am very pleased with him.

I will put my Spirit on him.

He will announce to the nations that everything

will be made right.

He will not argue or cry out.

No one will hear his voice in the streets.

He will not break a bent twig.

He will not put out a dimly burning flame.

He will make everything right.

The nations will put their hope in him."[1]

On one of those days, Jesus went out to a mountainside to pray. He spent the night praying to God. When morning came, he called for his disciples to come to him. He chose 12 of them and made them apostles.[2] From that time on they would be with him. He would also send them out to preach. He gave them authority to drive out evil spirits and to heal every illness and sickness.

Here are the names of the 12 apostles. First are Simon Peter and his brother Andrew. Then come James, son of Zebedee, and his brother John. Jesus gave them the name Boanerges. Boanerges means Sons of Thunder. Next are Philip and Bartholomew, and also Thomas and Matthew the tax collector. Two more are James, son of Alphaeus, and Thaddaeus. The last are Simon the Zealot and Judas Iscariot. Judas is the one who was later going to hand Jesus over to his enemies.[3]

Jesus went down the mountain with them and stood on a level place. A large crowd of his disciples was there. A large number of other people were there too.

They had all come to hear Jesus and to be healed of their sicknesses. People who were troubled by evil spirits were made well. Everyone tried to touch Jesus. Power was coming from him and healing them all.

Jesus saw the crowds. So he went up on a mountainside and sat down. His disciples came to him. Then he began to teach them.

He said,

"Blessed are those who are spiritually needy.

The kingdom of heaven belongs to them.

Blessed are those who are sad.

They will be comforted.

Blessed are those who are free of pride.

They will be given the earth.

Blessed are those who are hungry and thirsty for
    what is right.
  They will be filled.
Blessed are those who show mercy.
  They will be shown mercy.
Blessed are those whose hearts are pure.
  They will see God.
Blessed are those who make peace.
  They will be called sons of God.
Blessed are those who suffer for doing what is right.
  The kingdom of heaven belongs to them.

"Blessed are you when people make fun of you and hurt you because of me. You are also blessed when they tell all kinds of evil lies about you because of me.

"Blessed are you when people hate you, when they have nothing to do with you and say bad things about you, and when they treat your name as something evil. They do all this because you are followers of the Son of Man.

"Their people treated the prophets the same way long ago. When these things happen to you, be glad and jump for joy. You will receive many blessings in heaven.

"But how terrible it will be for you who are rich!
  You have already had your easy life.
How terrible for you who are well fed now!
  You will go hungry.
How terrible for you who laugh now!
  You will cry and be sad.
How terrible for you when everyone says good
    things about you!
  Their people treated the false prophets the same
    way long ago.

"You are the salt of the earth. But suppose the salt loses its saltiness. How can it be made salty again? It is no longer good for anything. It will be thrown out. People will walk all over it.

"You are the light of the world. A city on a hill can't be hidden. Also, people do not light a lamp and put it under a bowl. Instead, they put it on its stand. Then it gives light to everyone in the house.

"In the same way, let your light shine in front of others. Then they will see the good things you do. And they will praise your Father who is in heaven.

"Your eye is like a lamp for your body. Suppose your eyes are good. Then your whole body also is full of light. But suppose your eyes are bad. Then your body also is full of darkness. So make sure that the light inside you is not darkness.

"Suppose your whole body is full of light. And suppose no part of it is dark. Then your body will be completely lit up. It will be as when the light of a lamp shines on you.

"Do not think I have come to get rid of what is written in the Law or in the Prophets. I have not come to do that. Instead, I have come to give full meaning to what is written. What I'm about to tell you is true. Heaven and earth will disappear before the smallest letter disappears from the Law. Not even the smallest stroke of a pen will disappear from the Law until everything is completed.

"Do not break even one of the least important commandments. And do not teach others to break them. If you do, you will be called the least important person in the kingdom of heaven. Instead, practice and teach these commands. Then you will be called important in the kingdom of heaven.

"Here is what I tell you. You must be more godly than the Pharisees and the teachers of the law. If you are not, you will certainly not enter the kingdom of heaven.

"You have heard what was said to people who lived long ago. They were told, 'Do not commit murder.[4] Anyone who murders will be judged for it.' But here is what I tell you. Do not be angry with your brother. Anyone who is angry with his brother will be judged. Again, anyone who says to his brother, 'Raca,'[5] must stand trial in the Sanhedrin. But anyone who says, 'You fool!' will be in danger of the fire in hell.

"Suppose you are offering your gift at the altar. And you remember that your brother has something against you. Leave your gift in front of the altar. First go and make peace with your brother. Then come back and offer your gift.

"Suppose someone has a claim against you and is taking you to court. Settle the matter quickly. Do it while you are still with him on your way. If you don't, he may hand you over to the judge. The judge may hand you over to the officer. And you may be thrown into prison. What I'm about to tell you is true. You will not get out until you have paid the very last penny!

"You have heard that it was said, 'Do not commit adultery.'[6] But here is what I tell you. Do not even look at a woman in the wrong way. Anyone who does has already committed adultery with her in his heart.

"If your right eye causes you to sin, poke it out and throw it away. Your eye is only one part of your body. It is better to lose it than for your whole body to be thrown into hell.

"If your right hand causes you to sin, cut it off and throw it away. Your hand is only one part of your body. It is better to lose it than for your whole body to go into hell.

"It has been said, 'Suppose a man divorces his wife. If he does, he must give her a letter of divorce.'[7] But here is what I tell you. Anyone who divorces his wife causes her to commit adultery. And anyone who gets married to the divorced woman commits adultery. A man may divorce his wife only if she has not been faithful to him.

"Again, you have heard what was said to your people long ago. They were told, 'Do not break the promises you make to the Lord. Keep the oaths you have made to him.'[8] But here is what I tell you. Do not make any promises like that at all. Do not make them in the name of heaven. That is God's throne. Do not make them in the name of the earth. That is the stool for God's feet. Do not make them in the name of Jerusalem. That is the city of the Great King. And do not take an oath in the name of your head. You can't make even one hair white or black.

"Just let your 'Yes' mean 'Yes.' Let your 'No' mean 'No.' Anything more than this comes from the evil one.

"You have heard that it was said, 'An eye must be put out for an eye. A tooth must be knocked out for a tooth.'[9] But here is what I tell you. Do not fight against an evil person.

"Suppose someone hits you on your right cheek. Turn your other cheek to him also. Suppose someone takes you to court to get your shirt. Let him have your coat also. Suppose someone forces you to go one mile. Go two miles with him.

"Give to the one who asks you for something. Don't turn away from the one who wants to borrow something from you.

"You have heard that it was said, 'Love your neighbor.[10] Hate your enemy.' But here is what I tell you. Love your enemies. Pray for those who hurt you. Do good to those who hate you. Bless those who call down curses on you. Then you will be sons of your Father who is in heaven.

"He causes his sun to shine on evil people and good people. He sends rain on those who do right and those who don't.

"Suppose you love those who love you. Should anyone praise you for that? Even 'sinners' love those who love them. And suppose you do good to those who are good to you. Should anyone praise you for that? Even 'sinners' do that. And suppose you lend money to those who can pay you back. Should anyone praise you for that? Even a 'sinner' lends to 'sinners,' expecting them to pay everything back.

"But love your enemies. Do good to them. Lend to them without expecting to get anything back. Then you will receive a lot in return. And you will be sons of the Most High God. He is kind to people who are evil and are not thankful. So have mercy, just as your Father has mercy. So be perfect, just as your Father in heaven is perfect.

"Be careful not to do 'good works' in front of others. Don't do them to be seen by others. If you do, your Father in heaven will not reward you.

"When you give to needy people, do not announce it by having trumpets blown. Do not be like those who only pretend to be holy. They announce what they do in the synagogues and on the streets. They want to be honored by others. What I'm about to tell you is true. They have received their complete reward.

"When you give to the needy, don't let your left hand know what your right hand is doing. Then your giving will be done secretly. Your Father will reward you. He sees what you do secretly.

"When you pray, do not be like those who only pretend to be holy. They love to stand and pray in the synagogues and on the street corners. They want to be seen by others. What I'm about to tell you is true. They have received their complete reward.

"When you pray, go into your room. Close the door and pray to your Father, who can't be seen. He will reward you. Your Father sees what is done secretly.

"When you pray, do not keep talking on and on the way ungodly people do. They think they will be heard because they talk a lot. Do not be like them. Your Father knows what you need even before you ask him.

"This is how you should pray.

"'Our Father in heaven,

may your name be honored.

May your kingdom come.

May what you want to happen be done

on earth as it is done in heaven.

Give us today our daily bread.

Forgive us our sins,

just as we also have forgiven those who sin against us.

Keep us from falling into sin when we are tempted.

Save us from the evil one.'

"Forgive people when they sin against you. If you do, your Father who is in heaven will also forgive you. But if you do not forgive people their sins, your Father will not forgive your sins.

"When you go without eating, do not look gloomy like those who only pretend to be holy. They make their faces very sad. They want to show people they are fasting. What I'm about to tell you is true. They have received their complete reward.

"But when you go without eating, put olive oil on your head. Wash your face. Then others will not know that you are fasting. Only your Father, who can't be seen, will know it. He will reward you. Your Father sees what is done secretly.

"Do not put away riches for yourselves on earth. Moths and rust can destroy them. Thieves can break in and steal them. Instead, put away riches for yourselves in heaven. There, moths and rust do not destroy them. There, thieves do not break in and steal them. Your heart will be where your riches are.

"No one can serve two masters at the same time. He will hate one of them and love the other. Or he will be faithful to one and dislike the other. You can't serve God and Money at the same time.

"I tell you, do not worry. Don't worry about your life and what you will eat or drink. And don't worry about your body and what you will wear. Isn't there more to life than eating? Aren't there more important things for the body than clothes?

"Look at the birds of the air. They don't plant or gather crops. They don't put away crops in storerooms. But your Father who is in heaven feeds them. Aren't you worth much more than they are?

"Can you add even one hour to your life by worrying? You can't do that very little thing. So why worry about the rest?

"And why do you worry about clothes? See how the wild flowers grow. They don't work or make clothing. But here is what I tell you. Not even Solomon in all of his glory was dressed like one of those flowers.

"If that is how God dresses the wild grass, won't he dress you even better? After all, the grass is here only today. Tomorrow it is thrown into the fire. Your faith is so small!

"So don't worry. Don't say, 'What will we eat?' Or, 'What will we drink?' Or, 'What will we wear?' People who are ungodly run after all of those things. Your Father who is in heaven knows that you need them.

"But put God's kingdom first. Do what he wants you to do. Then all of those things will also be given to you.

"Little flock, do not be afraid. Your Father has been pleased to give you the kingdom. Sell what you own. Give to those who are poor. Provide purses for yourselves that will not wear out. Put away riches in heaven that will not be used up. There, no thief can come near it. There, no moth can destroy it. Your heart will be where your riches are.

"So don't worry about tomorrow. Tomorrow will worry about itself. Each day has enough trouble of its own.

"Do not judge others. Then you will not be judged. If you do not find others guilty, then you will not be found guilty. You will be measured in the same way you measure others. Forgive, and you will be forgiven.

"Give, and it will be given to you. A good amount will be poured into your lap. It will be pressed down, shaken together, and running over. The same amount you give will be measured out to you."

Jesus also gave them another example. He asked, "Can a blind person lead another blind person? Won't they both fall into a pit? Students are not better than their teachers. But everyone who is completely trained will be like his teacher.

"You look at the bit of sawdust in your friend's eye. But you pay no attention to the piece of wood in your own eye. How can you say to your friend, 'Let me take the bit of sawdust out of your eye'?

How can you say this while there is a piece of wood in your own eye?

"You pretender! First take the piece of wood out of your own eye. Then you will be able to see clearly to take the bit of sawdust out of your friend's eye.

"Do not give holy things to dogs. Do not throw your pearls to pigs. If you do, they might walk all over them. Then they might turn around and tear you to pieces.

"Ask, and it will be given to you. Search, and you will find. Knock, and the door will be opened to you. Everyone who asks will receive. He who searches will find. The door will be opened to the one who knocks.

"Suppose your son asks for bread. Which of you will give him a stone? Or suppose he asks for a fish. Which of you will give him a snake? Even though you are evil, you know how to give good gifts to your children. How much more will your Father who is in heaven give good gifts to those who ask him!

"In everything, do to others what you would want them to do to you. This is what is written in the Law and in the Prophets.

"Enter God's kingdom through the narrow gate. The gate is large and the road is wide that lead to death and hell. Many people go that way. But the gate is small and the road is narrow that lead to life. Only a few people find it.

"Watch out for false prophets. They come to you pretending to be sheep. But on the inside they are hungry wolves. You can tell what they really are by what they do.

"Do people pick grapes from bushes? Do they pick figs from thorns? In the same way, every good tree bears good fruit. But a bad tree bears bad fruit. A good tree can't bear bad fruit. And a bad tree can't bear good fruit. Every tree that does not bear good fruit is cut down. It is thrown into the fire. You can tell each tree by its fruit.

"A good man says good things. These come from the good that is put away in his heart. An evil man says evil things. These come from the evil that is put away in his heart. Their mouths say everything that is in their hearts.

"Not everyone who says to me, 'Lord, Lord,' will enter the kingdom of heaven. Only those who do what my Father in heaven wants will enter.

"Many will say to me on that day, 'Lord! Lord! Didn't we prophesy in your name? Didn't we drive out demons in your name? Didn't we do many miracles in your name?' Then I will tell them clearly, 'I never knew you. Get away from me, you who do evil!'

"Why do you call me, 'Lord, Lord,' and still don't do what I say? Some people come to me and listen to me and do what I say.

"So then, everyone who hears my words and puts them into practice is like a wise man. He builds his house on the rock. He digs down deep and sets it on solid rock. The rain comes down. The water rises. The winds blow and beat against that house. When a flood comes, the river rushes against the house. But it does not fall. It is built on the rock.

"But everyone who hears my words and does not put them into practice is like a foolish man. He builds his house on sand. The rain comes down. The water rises. The moment the river rushes against that house, it falls down. It is completely destroyed."

Jesus finished saying all these things. The crowds were amazed at his teaching. He taught like one who had authority. He did not speak like their teachers of the law.

chapter seven

Accused of Using Evil

Jesus finished saying all these things to the people. Then he entered Capernaum. There the servant of a Roman commander was sick and about to die. His master thought highly of him. The commander heard about Jesus. So he sent some elders of the Jews to him. He told them to ask Jesus to come and heal his servant.

They came to Jesus and begged him, "This man deserves to have you do this. He loves our nation and has built our synagogue."

Jesus said, "I will go and heal him." So Jesus went with them.

When Jesus came near the house, the Roman commander sent friends to him. He told them to say, "Lord, don't trouble yourself. I am not good enough to have you come into my house. That is why I did not even think I was fit to come to you. But just say the word, and my servant will be healed. I myself am a man who is under authority. And I have soldiers who obey my orders. I tell this one, 'Go,' and he goes. I tell that one, 'Come,' and he comes. I say to my servant, 'Do this,' and he does it."

When Jesus heard this, he was amazed at him. He turned to the crowd that was following him. He said, "I tell you, even in Israel I have not found anyone whose faith is so strong."

Then the men who had been sent to Jesus returned to the house. They found that the servant was healed.

Some time later, Jesus went to a town called Nain. His disciples and a large crowd went along with him. He approached the town gate. Just then, a dead person was being carried out. He was the only son of his mother. She was a widow. A large crowd from the town was with her.

When the Lord saw her, he felt sorry for her. So he said, "Don't cry."

Then he went up and touched the coffin. Those carrying it stood still.

Jesus said, "Young man, I say to you, get up!"

The dead man sat up and began to talk. Then Jesus gave him back to his mother.

The people were all filled with wonder and praised God. "A great prophet has appeared among us," they said. "God has come to help his people." This news about Jesus spread all through Judea and the whole country.

John was in prison. John's disciples told him about all these things. When he heard what Christ was doing, he sent his disciples to him.

The men came to Jesus. They said, "John the Baptist sent us to ask you, 'Are you the one who was supposed to come? Or should we look for someone else?'"

At that very time Jesus healed many people. They had illnesses, sicknesses and evil spirits. He also gave sight to many who were blind. So Jesus replied to the messengers, "Go back to John. Tell him what you have seen and heard. Blind people receive sight. Disabled people walk. Those who have skin diseases are healed. Deaf people hear. Those who are dead are raised to life. And the good news is preached to those who are poor. Blessed are those who do not give up their faith because of me."

So John's messengers left. Then Jesus began to speak to the crowd about John. He said, "What did you go out into the desert to see? Tall grass waving in the wind? If not, what did you go out to see? A man dressed in fine clothes? No. Those who wear fine clothes and have many expensive things are in palaces. Then what did you go out to see? A prophet? Yes, I tell you, and more than a prophet.

"He is the one written about in Scripture. It says,

"'I will send my messenger ahead of you.

He will prepare your way for you.'[1]

"What I'm about to tell you is true. No one more important than John the Baptist has ever been born. But the least important person in the kingdom of heaven is more important than he is. Since the days of John the Baptist, the kingdom of heaven has been advancing with force. And forceful people are taking hold of it. All the Prophets and the Law prophesied until John came. If you are willing to accept it, John is the Elijah who was supposed to come. Those who have ears should listen.

"What can I compare today's people to? They are like children sitting in the marketplaces and calling out to others. They say,

"'We played the flute for you.

But you didn't dance.

We sang a funeral song.

But you didn't become sad.'

"That is how it has been with John the Baptist. When he came to you, he didn't eat bread or drink wine. And you say, 'He has a demon.' But when the Son of Man came, he ate and drank as you do. And you say, 'This fellow is always eating and drinking far too much. He's a friend of tax collectors and "sinners."' Those who act wisely prove that wisdom is right."

All the people who heard Jesus' words agreed that God's way was right. Even the tax collectors agreed. These people had all been baptized by John. But the Pharisees and the authorities on the law did not accept God's purpose for themselves. They had not been baptized by John.

At that time Jesus said, "I praise you, Father. You are Lord of heaven and earth. You have hidden these things from the wise and educated. But you have shown them to little children. Yes, Father. This is what you wanted.

"My Father has given all things to me. The Father is the only one who knows the Son. And the only ones who know the Father are the Son and those to whom the Son chooses to make him known.

"Come to me, all of you who are tired and are carrying heavy loads. I will give you rest. Become my servants and learn from me. I am gentle and free of pride. You will find rest for your souls. Serving me is easy, and my load is light."

One of the Pharisees invited Jesus to have dinner with him. So he went to the Pharisee's house. He took his place at the table.

There was a woman in that town who had lived a sinful life. She learned that Jesus was eating at the Pharisee's house. So she came with a special sealed jar of perfume. She stood behind Jesus and cried at his feet. She began to wet his feet with her tears. Then she wiped them with her hair. She kissed them and poured perfume on them.

The Pharisee who had invited Jesus saw this. He said to himself, "If this man were a prophet, he would know who is touching him. He would know what kind of woman she is. She is a sinner!"

Jesus answered him, "Simon, I have something to tell you."

"Tell me, teacher," he said.

"Two people owed money to a certain lender. One owed him 500 silver coins. The other owed him 50 silver coins. Neither of them had the money to pay him back. So he let them go without paying. Which of them will love him more?"

Simon replied, "I suppose the one who owed the most money."

"You are right," Jesus said.

Then he turned toward the woman. He said to Simon, "Do you see this woman? I came into your house. You did not give me any water to wash my feet. But she wet my feet with her tears and wiped them with her hair. You did not give me a kiss. But this woman has not stopped kissing my feet since I came in. You did not put any olive oil on my head. But she has poured perfume on my feet. So I tell you this. Her many sins have been forgiven. She has loved a lot. But the one who has been forgiven little loves only a little."

Then Jesus said to her, "Your sins are forgiven."

The other guests began to talk about this among themselves. They said, "Who is this who even forgives sins?"

Jesus said to the woman, "Your faith has saved you. Go in peace."

After this, Jesus traveled around from one town and village to another. He announced the good news of God's kingdom. The Twelve were with him. So were some women who had been healed of evil spirits and sicknesses. One was Mary Magdalene. Seven demons had come out of her. Another was Joanna, the wife of Cuza. He was the manager of Herod's household. Susanna and many others were there also. These women were helping to support Jesus and the Twelve with their own money.

Jesus entered a house. Again a crowd gathered. It was so large that Jesus and his disciples were not even able to eat. His family heard about this. So they went to take charge of him. They said, "He is out of his mind."

A man controlled by demons was brought to Jesus. The man was blind and could not speak. Jesus healed him. Then the man could speak and see. All the people were amazed. They said, "Could this be the Son of David?"

Some teachers of the law were there. They had come down from Jerusalem. They said, "He is controlled by Beelzebub![2] This fellow drives out demons by the power of Beelzebub, the prince of demons."

Jesus knew what they were thinking. So he said to them, "Every kingdom that fights against itself will be destroyed. Every city or family that is divided against itself will not stand. If Satan drives out Satan, he fights against himself. Then how can his kingdom stand?

"I say this because of what you claim. You say I drive out demons by the power of Beelzebub. Suppose I do drive out demons with Beelzebub's help. With whose help do your followers drive them out?

So then, they will be your judges. But suppose I drive out demons with the help of God's powerful finger. Then God's kingdom has come to you.

"When a strong man is completely armed and guards his house, what he owns is safe. But when someone stronger attacks, he is overpowered. The attacker takes away the armor the man had trusted in. Then he divides up what he has stolen.

"Anyone who is not with me is against me. Anyone who does not gather sheep with me scatters them.

"What I'm about to tell you is true. Everyone's sins and evil words against God will be forgiven. Anyone who speaks a word against the Son of Man will be forgiven. But anyone who speaks against the Holy Spirit will not be forgiven. A person like that won't be forgiven either now or in days to come.

"You nest of poisonous snakes! How can you who are evil say anything good? Your mouths say everything that is in your hearts. A good man says good things. These come from the good that is put away inside him. An evil man says evil things. These come from the evil that is put away inside him. But here is what I tell you. On judgment day, people will have to account for every careless word they have spoken. By your words you will be found guilty or not guilty."

Jesus said this because the teachers of the law were saying, "He has an evil spirit."

As Jesus was saying these things, a woman in the crowd called out. She shouted, "Blessed is the mother who gave you birth and nursed you."

He replied, "Instead, blessed are those who hear God's word and obey it."

As the crowds grew larger, Jesus spoke to them. "The people of today are evil," he said. "They ask for a miraculous sign from God. But none will be given except the sign of the prophet Jonah.[3] He was a sign from God to the people of Nineveh. In the same way, the Son of Man will be a sign from God to the people of today. Jonah was in the stomach of a huge fish for three days and three nights. Something like that will happen to the Son of Man. He will spend three days and three nights in the grave.

"The men of Nineveh will stand up on judgment day with the people now living. And the Ninevites will prove that those people are guilty. The men of Nineveh turned away from their sins when Jonah preached to them. And now one who is more important than Jonah is here.

"The Queen of the South will stand up on judgment day with the people now living. And she will prove that they are guilty. She came from very far away to listen to Solomon's wisdom. And now one who is more important than Solomon is here.[4]

"What happens when an evil spirit comes out of a man? It goes through dry areas looking for a place to rest. But it doesn't find it. Then it says, 'I will return to the house I left.' When it arrives there, it finds the house empty. The house has been swept clean and put in order. Then the evil spirit goes and takes with it seven other spirits more evil than itself. They go in and live there. That man is worse off than before. That is how it will be with the evil people of today."

While Jesus was still talking to the crowd, his mother and brothers stood outside. They wanted to speak to him. But they could not get near him because of the crowd. They sent someone in to get him. A crowd was sitting around Jesus. Someone told him, "Your mother and your brothers are standing outside. They want to speak to you."

Jesus replied to him, "Who is my mother? And who are my brothers?"

Then Jesus looked at the people sitting in a circle around him. Jesus pointed to his disciples. He said, "Here is my mother! Here are my brothers! Anyone who does what my Father in heaven wants is my brother or sister or mother."

That same day Jesus left the house and sat by the Sea of Galilee.

People came to Jesus from town after town. The crowd that gathered around him was very large. So he got into a boat. He sat down in it out on the lake. All the people were along the shore at the water's edge. He taught them many things by using stories.

In his teaching he said, "Listen! A farmer went out to plant his seed. He scattered the seed on the ground. Some fell on a path. People walked on it, and the birds of the air ate it up. Some seed fell on rocky places, where there wasn't much soil. The plants came up quickly, because the soil wasn't deep. When the sun came up, it burned the plants. They dried up because they had no roots. Other seed fell among thorns. The thorns grew up and crowded out the plants. So the plants did not bear grain. Still other seed fell on good soil. It grew up and produced a crop 30, 60, or even 100 times more than the farmer planted."

Then Jesus said, "Those who have ears should listen."

Later Jesus was alone. The Twelve asked him about the stories. So did the others around him. They asked, "Why do you use stories when you speak to the people?"

He replied, "You have been given the chance to understand the secrets of the kingdom of heaven. It has not been given to outsiders. Everyone who has that kind of knowledge will be given more. In fact, they will have very much. If anyone doesn't have that kind of knowledge, even what little he has will be taken away from him.

"Here is why I use stories when I speak to the people. I say,

"They look, but they don't really see.

They listen, but they don't really hear or understand.

"In them the words of the prophet Isaiah come true. He said,

"'You will hear but never understand.

You will see but never know what you are seeing.

The hearts of these people have become stubborn.

They can barely hear with their ears.

They have closed their eyes.

Otherwise they might see with their eyes.

They might hear with their ears.

They might understand with their hearts.

They might turn to the Lord, and then he would
heal them.'[5]

"But blessed are your eyes because they see. And blessed are your ears because they hear. What I'm about to tell you is true. Many prophets and godly people wanted to see what you see. But they didn't see it. They wanted to hear what you hear. But they didn't hear it."

Then Jesus said to them, "Don't you understand this story? Then how will you understand any stories of this kind?

"Listen! Here is the meaning of the story of the farmer. The seed the farmer plants is God's message. What is seed scattered on a path like? The message is planted. People hear the message about the kingdom but do not understand it. Then the evil one comes. He steals what was planted in their hearts. He does it so they won't believe. Then they can't be saved.

"And what is seed scattered on rocky places like? The people hear the message. At once they receive it with joy. But they have no roots. So they last only a short time. They quickly fall away from the faith when trouble or suffering comes because of the message.

"And what is seed scattered among thorns like? The people hear the message. But then the worries of this life come to them. Wealth comes with its false promises. The people also long for other things. All of those are the kinds of things that crowd out the message. They keep it from producing fruit.

"And what is seed scattered on good soil like? The people hear the message. They accept it. They are those who hear the message and understand it. They produce a good crop 30, 60, or even 100 times more than the farmer planted."

Jesus said to them, "Do you bring in a lamp to put it under a large bowl or a bed? Don't you put it on its stand? Then those who come in can see its light. What is hidden will be seen. And what is out of sight will be brought into the open and made known.

"So be careful how you listen. If you have something, you will be given more. If you have nothing, even what you think you have will be taken away from you."

Jesus told the crowd another story. "Here is what the kingdom of heaven is like," he said. "A man planted good seed in his field. But while everyone was sleeping, his enemy came. The enemy planted weeds among the wheat and then went away. The wheat began to grow and form grain. At the same time, weeds appeared.

"The owner's servants came to him. They said, 'Sir, didn't you plant good seed in your field? Then where did the weeds come from?'

"'An enemy did this,' he replied.

"The servants asked him, 'Do you want us to go and pull the weeds up?'

"'No,' the owner answered. 'While you are pulling up the weeds, you might pull up the wheat with them. Let both grow together until the harvest. At that time I will tell the workers what to do. Here is what I will say to them. First collect the weeds. Tie them in bundles to be burned. Then gather the wheat. Bring it into my storeroom.'"

Jesus also said, "Here is what God's kingdom is like. A farmer scatters seed on the ground. Night and day the seed comes up and grows. It happens whether the farmer sleeps or gets up. He doesn't know how it happens. All by itself the soil produces grain. First the stalk comes up. Then the head appears. Finally, the full grain appears in the head. Before long the grain ripens. So the farmer cuts it down, because the harvest is ready."

Again Jesus said, "What can we say God's kingdom is like? What story can we use to explain it? It is like a mustard seed, which is the smallest seed planted in the ground. But when you plant the seed, it grows. It becomes the largest of all garden plants. Its branches are so big that birds can rest in its shade."

Again he asked, "What can I compare God's kingdom to? It is like yeast that a woman used. She mixed it into a large amount of flour. The yeast worked its way all through the dough."

Then Jesus left the crowd and went into the house. His disciples came to him. They said, "Explain to us the story of the weeds in the field."

He answered, "The one who planted the good seed is the Son of Man. The field is the world. The good seed stands for the people who belong to the kingdom. The weeds are the people who belong to the evil one. The enemy who plants them is the devil. The harvest is judgment day. And the workers are angels.

"The weeds are pulled up and burned in the fire. That is how it will be on judgment day. The Son of Man will send out his angels. They will weed out of his kingdom everything that causes sin. They will also get rid of all who do evil. They will throw them into the blazing furnace. There people will sob and grind their teeth. Then God's people will shine like the sun in their Father's kingdom. Those who have ears should listen.

"The kingdom of heaven is like treasure that was hidden in a field. When a man found it, he hid it again. He was very happy. So he went and sold everything he had. And he bought that field.

"Again, the kingdom of heaven is like a trader who was looking for fine pearls. He found one that was very valuable. So he went away and sold everything he had. And he bought that pearl.

"Again, the kingdom of heaven is like a net. It was let down into the lake. It caught all kinds of fish. When it was full, the fishermen pulled it up on the shore. Then they sat down and gathered the good fish into baskets. But they threw the bad fish away. This is how it will be on judgment day. The angels will come. They will separate the people who did what is wrong from those who did what is right. They will throw the evil people into the blazing furnace. There the evil ones will sob and grind their teeth. Do you understand all these things?" Jesus asked.

"Yes," they replied.

He said to them, "Every teacher of the law who has been taught about the kingdom of heaven is like the owner of a house. He brings new treasures out of his storeroom as well as old ones."

Using many stories like those, Jesus spoke the word to them. He told them as much as they could understand. He did not say anything to them without using a story. So the words spoken by the prophet came true. He had said,

"I will open my mouth and tell stories.

I will speak about things that were hidden since

the world was made."[6]

But when he was alone with his disciples, he explained everything.

chapter eight

Calming a Storm

When evening came, Jesus said to his disciples, "Let's go over to the other side of the lake." So they got into a boat and left. There were also other boats with him.

As they sailed, Jesus fell asleep. Suddenly a terrible storm came up on the lake. The waves crashed over the boat. It was so bad that the boat was about to sink. They were in great danger. Jesus was in the back, sleeping on a cushion.

The disciples went and woke Jesus up. They said, "Master! Master! We're going to drown! Teacher! Don't you care if we drown?"

He replied, "Your faith is so small! Why are you so afraid?"

He got up and ordered the wind to stop. He said to the waves, "Quiet! Be still!" Then the wind died down. And it was completely calm.

He said to his disciples, "Why are you so afraid? Don't you have any faith at all yet?"

They were amazed and full of fear. They asked one another, "Who is this? He commands even the winds and the waves and they obey him."

Jesus and his disciples sailed to the area of the Gerasenes across the lake from Galilee. When Jesus stepped on shore, he was met by a man from the town.[1] The man was controlled by demons. For a long time he had not worn clothes or lived in a house. The man lived in the tombs.

No one could keep him tied up anymore. Not even a chain could hold him. His hands and feet had often been chained. But he tore the chains apart. And he broke the iron cuffs on his ankles. And then the demon had forced him to go out into lonely places in the countryside. No one was strong enough to control him. Night and day he screamed among the tombs and in the hills. He cut himself with stones.

When he saw Jesus a long way off, he ran to him. He fell on his knees in front of him. He shouted at the top of his voice, "Jesus, Son of the Most High God, what do you want with me? Promise before God that you won't hurt me!" This was because Jesus had said to him, "Come out of this man, you evil spirit!"

Then Jesus asked the demon, "What is your name?"

"My name is Legion," he replied. "There are many of us."

And they begged Jesus again and again not to order them to go into the Abyss.[2]

A large herd of pigs was feeding there on the nearby hillside. The demons begged Jesus, "If you drive us out, send us into the herd of pigs."

Jesus said to them, "Go!"

The evil spirits came out of the man and went into the pigs. There were about 2,000 pigs in the herd. The whole herd rushed down the steep bank. They ran into the lake and drowned.

Those who were tending the pigs ran off. They told the people in the town and countryside what had happened.

The people went out to see for themselves.

Then they came to Jesus. They saw the man who had been controlled by many demons. He was sitting at Jesus' feet. He was now dressed and thinking clearly. All this made the people afraid.

Those who had seen it told the others how the man who had been controlled by demons was now healed. They told about the pigs as well. Then the people began to beg Jesus to leave their area. They were filled with fear.

Jesus was getting into the boat. The man who had been controlled by demons begged to go with him. Jesus did not let him. He said, "Go home to your family. Tell them how much the Lord has done for you. Tell them how kind he has been to you."

So the man went away. He told people all over town how much Jesus had done for him. And all the people were amazed.

Jesus stepped into a boat. He went over to the other side of the lake and came to his own town. There a large crowd gathered around him. They were all expecting him.

Then a man named Jairus came. He was a synagogue ruler. He fell at Jesus' feet. His only daughter was dying. She was about 12 years old. He begged Jesus, "Please come. My little daughter is dying. Place your hands on her to heal her. Then she will live." Jesus got up and went with him. So did his disciples.

As Jesus was on his way, the crowds almost crushed him.

A woman was there who had a sickness that made her bleed. Her sickness had lasted for 12 years. No one could heal her. She had suffered a great deal, even though she had gone to many doctors. She had spent all the money she had. But she was getting worse, not better. Then she heard about Jesus. She thought, "I only need to touch his clothes. Then I will be healed."

She came up behind him in the crowd and touched his clothes. Right away her bleeding stopped. She felt in her body that her suffering was over.

At once Jesus knew that power had gone out from him. He turned around in the crowd. He asked, "Who touched my clothes?"

They all said they didn't do it. Then Peter said, "Master, the people are crowding and pushing against you. And you still ask, 'Who touched me?'"

But Jesus said, "Someone touched me. I know that power has gone out from me."

Jesus kept looking around. He wanted to see who had touched him.

Then the woman came and fell at his feet. She knew what had happened to her. She was shaking with fear. But she told him the whole truth. In front of everyone, she told why she had touched him. She also told how she had been healed in an instant.

He said to her, "Dear woman, your faith has healed you. Go in peace. You are free from your suffering."

While Jesus was still speaking, some people came from the house of Jairus. "Your daughter is dead," they said. "Why bother the teacher anymore?"

But Jesus didn't listen to them. He told the synagogue ruler, "Don't be afraid. Just believe. She will be healed."

When he arrived at the house of Jairus, he did not let everyone go in with him. He took only Peter, John and James, and the child's father and mother.

During this time, all the people were crying and sobbing loudly over the child.

When Jesus entered the ruler's house, he saw the flute players there. And he saw the noisy crowd. Then he said to them, "Why all this confusion and sobbing? Go away. Stop crying! She is not dead. She is sleeping."

But they laughed at him. They knew she was dead.

He made them all go outside. He took only the child's father and mother and the disciples who were with him. And he went in where the child was. He took her by the hand. Then he said to her, "Talitha koum!" This means (in Aramaic), "Little girl, I say to you, get up!"

Her spirit returned, and right away she stood up. They were totally amazed at this. Then Jesus told them to give her something to eat.

Jesus ordered them not to tell anyone what had happened. But news about what Jesus had done spread all over that area.

As Jesus went on from there, two blind men followed him. They called out, "Have mercy on us, Son of David!"

When Jesus went indoors, the blind men came to him. He asked them, "Do you believe that I can do this?"

"Yes, Lord," they replied.

Then he touched their eyes. He said, "It will happen to you just as you believed." They could now see again. Jesus strongly warned them, "Be sure that no one knows about this." But they went out and spread the news. They talked about him all over that area.

While they were going out, another man was brought to Jesus. A demon controlled him, and he could not speak. When the demon was driven out, the man spoke.

The crowd was amazed. They said, "Nothing like this has ever been seen in Israel." But the Pharisees said, "He drives out demons by the power of the prince of demons."

Jesus left there and went to his hometown of Nazareth. His disciples went with him. When the Sabbath day came, he began to teach in the synagogue. Many who heard him were amazed.

"Where did this man get these things?" they asked. "What's this wisdom that has been given to him? He even does miracles! Isn't this the carpenter? Isn't this Mary's son? Isn't this the brother of James, Joseph, Judas and Simon? Aren't his sisters here with us?" They were not pleased with him at all.

Jesus said to them, "A prophet is not honored in his hometown. He doesn't receive any honor among his relatives. And he doesn't receive any in his own home."

Jesus laid his hands on a few sick people and healed them. But he could not do any other miracles there. He was amazed because they had no faith.

Jesus went through all the towns and villages. He taught in their synagogues. He preached the good news of the kingdom. And he healed every illness and sickness. When he saw the crowds, he felt deep concern for them. They were beaten down and helpless, like sheep without a shepherd.

Then Jesus said to his disciples, "The harvest is huge. But there are only a few workers. So ask the Lord of the harvest to send workers out into his harvest field."

Jesus called the Twelve together. He gave them power and authority to drive out all demons and to heal sicknesses. Then he sent them out to preach about God's kingdom and to heal those who were sick. He sent them out two by two.

Here were his orders. "Do not go among those who aren't Jews," he said. "Do not enter any town of the Samaritans. Instead, go to the people of Israel. They are like sheep that have become lost. As you go, preach this message, 'The kingdom of heaven is near.' Heal those who are sick. Bring those who are dead back to life. Make those who have skin diseases 'clean' again. Drive out demons. You have received freely, so give freely.

"Don't take anything for the journey. Do not take along any gold, silver or copper in your belts. Do not take bread or a bag. Do not take extra clothes or sandals or walking sticks. A worker should be given what he needs.

"When you enter a town or village, look for someone who is willing to welcome you. Stay at that person's house until you leave. As you enter the home, greet those who live there. If that home welcomes you, give it your blessing of peace. If it does not, don't bless it.

"Some people may not welcome you or listen to your words. If they don't, shake the dust off your feet when you leave that home or town. That will be a witness against the people living there. What I'm about to tell you is true. On judgment day it will be easier for Sodom and Gomorrah[3] than for that town.

"I am sending you out like sheep among wolves. So be as wise as snakes and as harmless as doves.

"Watch out! Men will hand you over to the local courts. They will whip you in their synagogues. You will be brought to governors and kings because of me. You will be witnesses to them and to those who aren't Jews.

"But when they arrest you, don't worry about what you will say or how you will say it. At that time you will be given the right words to say. It will not be you speaking. The Spirit of your Father will be speaking through you.

"Brothers will hand over brothers to be killed. Fathers will hand over their children. Children will rise up against their parents and have them put to death. Everyone will hate you because of me. But anyone who stands firm to the end will be saved.

"When people attack you in one place, escape to another. What I'm about to tell you is true. You will not finish going through the cities of Israel before the Son of Man comes.

"A student is not better than his teacher. A servant is not better than his master. It is enough for the student to be like his teacher. And it is enough for the servant to be like his master. If the head of the house has been called Beelzebub, what can the others who live there expect?

"So don't be afraid of your enemies. Everything that is secret will be brought out into the open. Everything that is hidden will be uncovered. What I tell you in the dark, speak in the daylight. What is whispered in your ear, shout from the rooftops.

"My friends, listen to me. Do not be afraid of those who kill the body but can't kill the soul. Instead, be afraid of the One who can destroy both soul and body in hell.

"Aren't two sparrows sold for only a penny? Aren't five sparrows sold for two pennies? But God does not forget even one of them. Not one of them falls to the ground without your Father knowing it. He even counts every hair on your head! So don't be afraid. You are worth more than many sparrows.

"What about someone who says in front of others that he knows me? I tell you, the Son of Man will say that he knows that person in front of God's angels. I will also say in front of my Father who is in heaven that I know him. But what about someone who says in front of others that he doesn't know me? I, the Son of Man, will say that I don't know him in front of God's angels. I will say in front of my Father who is in heaven that I don't know him.

"I have come to bring fire on the earth. How I wish the fire had already started! But I have a baptism of suffering to go through. And I will be very troubled until it is completed.

"Do you think I came to bring peace on earth? No, I tell you. I have come to separate people. I didn't come to bring peace. I came to bring a sword. I have come to turn

"'Sons against their fathers.

Daughters will refuse to obey their mothers.

Daughters-in-law will be against their mothers-in-law.

A man's enemies will be the members of his own

family.'[4]

"From now on there will be five members in a family, each one against the other. There will be three against two and two against three. They will be separated. Father will turn against son and son against father. Mother will turn against daughter and daughter against mother. Mother-in-law will turn against daughter-in-law and daughter-in-law against mother-in-law.

"Anyone who loves his father or mother more than me is not worthy of me. Anyone who loves his son or daughter more than me is not worthy of me. And anyone who does not pick up his cross and follow me is not worthy of me. If anyone finds his life, he will lose it. If anyone loses his life because of me, he will find it.

"Anyone who welcomes you welcomes me. And anyone who welcomes me welcomes the One who sent me. Suppose someone welcomes a prophet as a prophet. That one will receive a prophet's reward. And suppose someone welcomes a godly person as a godly person. That one will receive a godly person's reward. Suppose someone gives even a cup of cold water to a little one who follows me. What I'm about to tell you is true. That one will certainly be rewarded."

Jesus finished teaching his 12 disciples. Then he went on to teach and preach in the towns of Galilee.

So the Twelve left. They went from village to village. And they preached that people should turn away from their sins. They drove out many demons. They poured olive oil on many sick people and healed them.

Now Herod, the ruler of Galilee, heard about everything that was going on. Jesus' name had become well known. He was bewildered, because some were saying that John the Baptist had been raised from the dead!

Others were saying that Elijah had appeared. Still others were saying that a prophet of long ago had come back to life.

But when Herod heard this, he said, "I had John's head cut off. And now he has been raised from the dead! So who is it that I hear such things about?" And he tried to see Jesus.

In fact, it was Herod himself who had given orders to arrest John. He had him tied up and put in prison. He did this because of Herodias. She was the wife of Herod's brother Philip. But now Herod was married to her. John had been saying to Herod, "It is against the Law for you to have your brother's wife." Herodias held that against John. She wanted to kill him. But she could not, because Herod was afraid of John. So he kept John safe. Herod knew John was a holy man who did what was right. When Herod heard him, he was very puzzled. But he liked to listen to him.

Finally the right time came. Herod gave a big dinner on his birthday. He invited his high officials and military leaders. He also invited the most important men in Galilee. Then the daughter of Herodias came in and danced. She pleased Herod and his dinner guests.

The king said to the girl, "Ask me for anything you want. I'll give it to you." And he promised her with an oath, "Anything you ask for I will give you. I'll give you up to half of my kingdom."

She went out and said to her mother, "What should I ask for?"

"The head of John the Baptist," she answered.

At once the girl hurried to ask the king. She said, "I want you to give me the head of John the Baptist on a big plate right now."

The king was very upset. But he thought of his promise and his dinner guests. So he did not want to say no to the girl. He sent a man right away to bring John's head. The man went to the prison and cut off John's head. He brought it back on a big plate. He gave it to the girl, and she gave it to her mother.

John's disciples came and took his body and buried it. Then they went and told Jesus.

chapter nine

Feeding the Hungry Crowds

Jesus heard what had happened to John. He wanted to be alone. The apostles gathered around Jesus. They told him all they had done and taught. But many people were coming and going. So they did not even have a chance to eat.

Then Jesus said to his apostles, "Come with me by yourselves to a quiet place. You need to get some rest." So they went away by themselves in a boat to a quiet place.

But many people who saw them leaving recognized them. They had seen the miraculous signs he had done on those who were sick. They ran from all the towns and got there ahead of them.

When Jesus came ashore, he saw a large crowd. He felt deep concern for them. They were like sheep without a shepherd. He welcomed them and spoke to them about God's kingdom. He also healed those who needed to be healed.

Then Jesus went up on a mountainside. There he sat down with his disciples. The Jewish Passover Feast was near.

When it was almost evening, the disciples came to him. "There is nothing here," they said. "It's already getting late. Send the crowd away. They can go and buy some food in the villages."

Jesus replied, "They don't need to go away. You give them something to eat."

Jesus looked up and saw a large crowd coming toward him. So he said to Philip, "Where can we buy bread for these people to eat?" He asked this only to put Philip to the test. He already knew what he was going to do.

Philip answered him, "Eight months' pay would not buy enough bread for each one to have a bite! Should we go and spend that much on bread? Are we supposed to feed them?"

"How many loaves do you have?" Jesus asked. "Go and see."

Another of his disciples spoke up. It was Andrew, Simon Peter's brother. He said, "Here is a boy with five small loaves of barley bread. He also has two small fish. But how far will that go in this large crowd? We would have to go and buy food for all this crowd."

"Bring them here to me," he said.

Then Jesus directed them to have all the people sit down in groups on the green grass. So they sat down in groups of 100s and 50s.

Jesus took the five loaves and the two fish. He looked up to heaven and gave thanks. He broke the loaves into pieces. Then he gave them to his disciples to set in front of the people. He gave them as much as they wanted. And he did the same with the fish.

All of them ate and were satisfied. The number of men who ate was about 5,000. Women and children also ate.

When all of them had enough to eat, Jesus spoke to his disciples. "Gather the leftover pieces," he said. "Don't waste anything."

So they gathered what was left over from the five barley loaves. They filled 12 baskets with the pieces left by those who had eaten.

The people saw the miraculous sign that Jesus did. Then they began to say, "This must be the Prophet who is supposed to come into the world." But Jesus knew that they planned to come and force him to be their king.

Right away Jesus made the disciples get into the boat. He had them go ahead of him to the other side of the Sea of Galilee. Then he sent the crowd away. After he had sent them away, he went up on a mountainside by himself to pray.

When evening came, the boat was in the middle of the Sea of Galilee. By now it was dark. Jesus had not yet joined them. He was alone on land.

A strong wind was blowing, and the water became rough. The boat was already a long way from land. It was being pounded by the waves because the wind was blowing against it. He saw the disciples pulling hard on the oars. They rowed three or three and a half miles.

Early in the morning, Jesus went out to the disciples. He walked on the lake. When he was about to pass by them, they saw him walking on the lake. They thought he was a ghost. They cried out. They all saw him and were terrified.

Right away Jesus called out to them, "Be brave! It is I. Don't be afraid."

"Lord, is it you?" Peter asked. "If it is, tell me to come to you on the water."

"Come," Jesus said.

So Peter got out of the boat. He walked on the water toward Jesus. But when Peter saw the wind, he was afraid. He began to sink. He cried out, "Lord! Save me!"

Right away Jesus reached out his hand and caught him. "Your faith is so small!" he said. "Why did you doubt me?"

When they climbed into the boat, the wind died down. Then those in the boat worshiped Jesus. They said, "You really are the Son of God!" And they were completely amazed. They had not understood about the loaves. They were stubborn.

Right away the boat reached the shore where they were heading. They crossed over the lake and landed at Gennesaret. There they tied up the boat.

As soon as Jesus and his disciples got out, people recognized him. They ran through that whole area to bring him those who were sick. They carried them on mats to where they heard he was.

He went into the villages, the towns, and the countryside. Everywhere he went, the people brought the sick to the market-places. Those who were sick begged him to let them just touch the edge of his clothes. And all who touched him were healed.

The next day the crowd that had stayed on the other side of the lake realized something. They saw that only one boat had been there. They knew that Jesus had not gotten into it with his disciples. And they knew that the disciples had gone away alone.

Then some boats from Tiberias landed. It was near the place where the people had eaten the bread after the Lord gave thanks. The crowd realized that Jesus and his disciples were not there. So they got into boats and went to Capernaum to look for Jesus.

They found him on the other side of the lake. They asked him, "Rabbi, when did you get here?"

Jesus answered, "What I'm about to tell you is true. You are not looking for me because you saw miraculous signs. You are looking for me because you ate the loaves until you were full. Do not work for food that spoils. Work for food that lasts forever. That is the food the Son of Man will give you. God the Father has put his seal of approval on him."

Then they asked him, "What does God want from us? What works does he want us to do?"

Jesus answered, "God's work is to believe in the One he has sent."

So they asked him, "What miraculous sign will you give us? What will you do so we can see it and believe you? Long ago our people ate the manna in the desert. It is written in Scripture, 'The Lord gave them bread from heaven to eat.'"[1]

Jesus said to them, "What I'm about to tell you is true. It is not Moses who has given you the bread from heaven. It is my Father who gives you the true bread from heaven. The bread of God is the One who comes down from heaven. He gives life to the world."

"Sir," they said, "give us this bread from now on."

Then Jesus said, "I am the bread of life. No one who comes to me will ever go hungry. And no one who believes in me will ever be thirsty.

"But it is just as I told you. You have seen me, and you still do not believe. Everyone the Father gives me will come to me. I will never send away anyone who comes to me.

"I have not come down from heaven to do what I want to do. I have come to do what the One who sent me wants me to do. The One who sent me doesn't want me to lose anyone he has given me. He wants me to raise them up on the last day. My Father wants all who look to the Son and believe in him to have eternal life. I will raise them up on the last day."

Then the Jews began to complain about Jesus. That was because he said, "I am the bread that came down from heaven." They said, "Isn't this Jesus, the son of Joseph? Don't we know his father and mother? How can he now say, 'I came down from heaven'?"

"Stop complaining among yourselves," Jesus answered. "No one can come to me unless the Father who sent me brings him. Then I will raise him up on the last day.

"It is written in the Prophets, 'God will teach all of them.'[2] Everyone who listens to the Father and learns from him comes to me.

"No one has seen the Father except the One who has come from God. Only he has seen the Father. What I'm about to tell you is true. Everyone who believes has life forever.

"I am the bread of life. Long ago your people ate the manna in the desert, and they still died. But here is the bread that comes down from heaven. A person can eat it and not die. I am the living bread that came down from heaven. Everyone who eats some of this bread will live forever. The bread is my body. I will give it for the life of the world."

Then the Jews began to argue sharply among themselves. They said, "How can this man give us his body to eat?"

Jesus said to them, "What I'm about to tell you is true. You must eat the Son of Man's body and drink his blood. If you don't, you have no life in you. Anyone who eats my body and drinks my blood has eternal life. I will raise him up on the last day.

"My body is real food. My blood is real drink. Anyone who eats my body and drinks my blood remains in me. And I remain in him.

"The living Father sent me, and I live because of him. In the same way, those who feed on me will live because of me. This is the bread that came down from heaven. Long ago your people ate manna and died. But those who feed on this bread will live forever."

He said this while he was teaching in the synagogue in Capernaum.

Jesus' disciples heard this. Many of them said, "This is a hard teaching. Who can accept it?"

Jesus was aware that his disciples were complaining about his teaching. So he said to them, "Does this upset you? What if you see the Son of Man go up to where he was before? The Holy Spirit gives life. The body means nothing at all. The words I have spoken to you are from the Spirit. They give life. But there are some of you who do not believe."

Jesus had known from the beginning which of them did not believe. And he had known who was going to hand him over to his enemies. So he continued speaking. He said, "This is why I told you that no one can come to me unless the Father helps him."

From this time on, many of his disciples turned back. They no longer followed him.

"You don't want to leave also, do you?" Jesus asked the Twelve.

Simon Peter answered him, "Lord, who can we go to? You have the words of eternal life. We believe and know that you are the Holy One of God."

Then Jesus replied, "Didn't I choose you, the Twelve? But one of you is a devil!" He meant Judas, the son of Simon Iscariot. Judas was one of the Twelve. But later he was going to hand Jesus over to his enemies.

Some Pharisees and some teachers of the law came from Jerusalem to see Jesus. They saw some of his disciples eating food with "unclean" hands. They asked, "Why don't your disciples obey what the elders teach? Your disciples don't wash their hands before they eat!"

(The Pharisees and all the Jews do not eat unless they wash their hands to make them pure. That's what the elders teach. When they come from the marketplace, they do not eat unless they wash. And they follow many other teachings. For example, they wash cups, pitchers, and kettles in a special way.[3])

Jesus replied, "And why don't you obey God's command? You would rather follow your own teachings! Isaiah was right. He prophesied about you people who pretend to be good. He said,

"'These people honor me by what they say.

But their hearts are far away from me.

Their worship doesn't mean anything to me.

They teach nothing but human rules.'[4]

You have let go of God's commands. And you are holding on to the teaching that men made up."

Jesus then said to them, "You have a fine way of setting aside God's commands! You do this so you can follow your own teachings. Moses said, 'Honor your father and mother.'[5] He also said, 'If anyone calls down a curse on his father or mother, he will be put to death.'[6] But you allow people to say to their parents, 'Any help you might have received from us is Corban.' (Corban means 'a gift set apart for God.') So you no longer let them do anything for their parents.

"You make the word of God useless by putting your own teachings in its place. And you do many things like that."

Again Jesus called the crowd to him. He said, "Listen to me, everyone. Understand this. What goes into your mouth does not make you 'unclean.' It's what comes out of your mouth that makes you 'unclean.'"

Then he left the crowd and entered the house. His disciples

asked him about this teaching. They asked, "Do you know that the Pharisees were angry when they heard this?"

Jesus replied, "There are plants that my Father in heaven has not planted. They will be pulled up by the roots. Leave them. The Pharisees are blind guides. If a blind person leads another who is blind, both of them will fall into a pit."

Peter said, "Explain this to us."

"Don't you understand yet?" Jesus asked them. "Don't you see? Nothing that enters people from the outside can make them 'unclean.' It doesn't go into the heart. It goes into the stomach. Then it goes out of the body." In saying this, Jesus was calling all foods "clean."[7]

He went on to say, "What comes out of people makes them 'unclean.' Things that come out of the mouth come from the heart. Those are the things that make you 'unclean.' Evil thoughts come from the inside, from people's hearts. So do sexual sins, stealing and murder. Adultery, greed, hate and cheating come from people's hearts too. So do desires that are not pure, and wanting what belongs to others. And so do telling lies about others and being proud and being foolish. All those evil things come from inside a person. They make him 'unclean.' But eating without washing your hands does not make you 'unclean.'"

Jesus went from there to a place near Tyre. He entered a house. He did not want anyone to know where he was. But he could not keep it a secret.

Soon a woman heard about him. An evil spirit controlled her little daughter. The woman came to Jesus and fell at his feet. She was a Greek, born in Syrian Phoenicia. She begged Jesus to drive the demon out of her daughter. She cried out, "Lord! Son of David! Have mercy on me! A demon controls my daughter. She is suffering terribly."

Jesus did not say a word. So his disciples came to him. They begged him, "Send her away. She keeps crying out after us."

Jesus answered, "I was sent only to the people of Israel. They are like lost sheep."

Then the woman fell to her knees in front of him. "Lord! Help me!" she said.

"First let the children eat all they want," he told her. "It is not right to take the children's bread and throw it to their dogs."

"Yes, Lord," she said. "But even the dogs eat the crumbs that fall from their owners' table."

Then Jesus answered, "Woman, you have great faith! That was a good reply. You may go. The demon has left your daughter." And her daughter was healed at that very moment.

So she went home and found her child lying on the bed. And the demon was gone.

Then Jesus left the area of Tyre and went through Sidon. He went down to the Sea of Galilee and into the area known as the Ten Cities. Then he went up on a mountainside and sat down. Large crowds came to him. They brought blind people and those who could not walk. They also brought disabled people, those who could not speak, and many others. They laid them at his feet, and he healed them.

There some people brought a man to him. The man was deaf and could hardly speak. They begged Jesus to place his hand on him.

Jesus took the man to one side, away from the crowd. He put his fingers into the man's ears. Then he spit and touched the man's tongue. Jesus looked up to heaven. With a deep sigh, he said to the man, "Ephphatha!" That means "Be opened!" The man's ears were opened. His tongue was freed up, and he began to speak clearly.

Jesus ordered the people not to tell anyone. But the more he did so, the more they kept talking about it.

People were really amazed. Those who could not speak were speaking. The disabled were made well. Those not able to walk were walking. Those who were blind could see. "He has done every-thing well," they said. "He even makes deaf people able to hear. And he makes those who can't speak able to talk." So the people praised the God of Israel.

During those days another large crowd gathered. They had nothing to eat. So Jesus called for his disciples to come to him. He said, "I feel deep concern for these people. They have already been with me three days. They don't have anything to eat. If I send them away hungry, they will become too weak on their way home. Some of them have come from far away."

His disciples answered him. "There is nothing here," they said. "Where could we get enough bread to feed this large crowd?"

"How many loaves do you have?" Jesus asked.

"Seven," they replied, "and a few small fish."

Jesus told the crowd to sit down on the ground. He took the seven loaves and the fish and gave thanks. Then he broke them and gave them to the disciples. He told the disciples to pass them around. The people ate and were satisfied. After that, the disciples picked up seven baskets of leftover pieces. The number of men who ate was 4,000. Women and children also ate.

After Jesus had sent the crowd away, he got into a boat. He went to the area near Magadan.

The Pharisees and Sadducees came to put Jesus to the test. They asked him to show them a miraculous sign from heaven.

He sighed deeply. He said, "Why do you people ask for a sign? What I'm about to tell you is true. No sign will be given to you.

"In the evening you look at the sky. You say, 'It will be good weather. The sky is red.' And in the morning you say, 'Today it will be stormy. The sky is red and cloudy.' You know the meaning of what you see in the sky. But you can't understand the signs of what is happening right now. An evil and unfaithful people look for a miraculous sign. But none will be given to them except the sign of Jonah."

Then he left them. He got back into the boat and crossed to the other side of the lake.

The disciples had forgotten to bring bread. They had only one loaf with them in the boat.

"Be careful," Jesus warned them. "Watch out for the yeast of the Pharisees. And watch out for the yeast of Herod."

The disciples talked about this among themselves. They said, "He must be saying this because we didn't bring any bread."

Jesus knew what they were saying. So he said, "Your faith is so small! Why are you talking to each other about having no bread? Why can't you see or understand? Are you stubborn? Do you have eyes and still don't see? Do you have ears and still don't hear? And don't you remember? Earlier I broke five loaves for the 5,000. How many baskets of pieces did you pick up?"

"Twelve," they replied.

"Later I broke seven loaves for the 4,000. How many baskets of pieces did you pick up?"

"Seven," they answered.

He said to them, "How can you possibly not understand? I wasn't talking to you about bread. But watch out for the yeast of the Pharisees and Sadducees."

Then the disciples understood that Jesus was not telling them to watch out for the yeast used in bread. He was warning them against what the Pharisees and Sadducees taught.

chapter ten

Seen in God's Glory

Jesus and his disciples came to Bethsaida. Some people brought a blind man. They begged Jesus to touch him.

He took the blind man by the hand. Then he led him outside the village. He spit on the man's eyes and put his hands on him.

"Do you see anything?" Jesus asked.

The man looked up. He said, "I see people. They look like trees walking around."

Once more Jesus put his hands on the man's eyes. Then his eyes were opened so that he could see again. He saw everything clearly.

Jesus sent him home. He told him, "Don't go into the village."

Jesus and his disciples went on to the villages around Caesarea Philippi. One day Jesus was praying alone. Only his disciples were with him. He asked them, "Who do the crowds say that I am?"

They replied, "Some say John the Baptist. Others say Elijah. Still others say that one of the prophets of long ago has come back to life."

"But what about you?" he asked. "Who do you say that I am?"

Simon Peter answered, "You are the Christ. You are the Son of the living God."

Jesus replied, "Blessed are you, Simon, son of Jonah! No mere man showed this to you. My Father in heaven showed it to you. Here is what I tell you. You are Peter. [1] On this rock I will build my church. The gates of hell will not be strong enough to destroy it. I will give you the keys to the kingdom of heaven. What you lock on earth will be locked in heaven. What you unlock on earth will be unlocked in heaven."

Then Jesus warned his disciples not to tell anyone that he was the Christ.

From that time on Jesus began to explain to his disciples what would happen to him. He told them he must go to Jerusalem. There he must suffer many things from the elders, the chief priests and the teachers of the law. He must be killed and on the third day rise to life again.

Peter took Jesus to one side and began to scold him. "Never, Lord!" he said. "This will never happen to you!"

Jesus turned and said to Peter, "Get behind me, Satan! You are standing in my way. You do not have in mind the things of God. Instead, you are thinking about human things."

Jesus called the crowd to him along with his disciples. Then he said to all of them, "If anyone wants to follow me, he must say no to himself. He must pick up his cross every day and follow me. [2] If he wants to save his life, he will lose it. But if he loses his life for me and for the good news, he will save it.

"What good is it if someone gains the whole world but loses his soul? Or what can anyone trade for his soul?

"Suppose you are ashamed of me and my words among these adulterous and sinful people. Then the Son of Man will be ashamed of you when he comes in his Father's glory with the holy angels. And he will reward everyone in keeping with what they have done.

"What I'm about to tell you is true. Some who are standing here will not die before they see the Son of Man coming in his kingdom."

After six days Jesus took Peter, James, and John with him. He led them up a high mountain. They were all alone.

There in front of them his appearance was changed. His face shone like the sun. His clothes became so white they shone. They were whiter than anyone in the world could bleach them. Two men, Moses and Elijah, appeared in shining glory. Jesus and the two of them talked together. They spoke about his coming death. He was going to die soon in Jerusalem.

Peter and his companions had been very sleepy. But then they became completely awake. They saw Jesus' glory and the two men standing with him.

Peter said to Jesus, "Lord, it is good for us to be here. If you wish, I will put up three shelters. One will be for you, one for Moses, and one for Elijah." Peter didn't really know what to say, because they were so afraid.

While Peter was still speaking, a bright cloud surrounded them. The disciples were afraid as they entered the cloud. A voice came from the cloud. It said, "This is my Son, and I love him. I am very pleased with him. Listen to him!"

When the disciples heard this, they were terrified. They fell with their faces to the ground. But Jesus came and touched them. "Get up," he said. "Don't be afraid."

They looked around. Suddenly they no longer saw anyone with them except Jesus.

They came down the mountain. On the way down, Jesus ordered them not to tell anyone what they had seen. He told them to wait until the Son of Man had risen from the dead.

So they kept the matter to themselves. They didn't tell anyone at that time what they had seen. But they asked each other what "rising from the dead" meant.

Then they asked Jesus, "Why do the teachers of the law say that Elijah has to come first?"

Jesus replied, "That's right. Elijah does come first. He makes all things new again. So why is it written that the Son of Man must suffer much and not be accepted? I tell you, Elijah has come. They have done to him everything they wanted to do. They did it just as it is written about him. In the same way, they are going to make the Son of Man suffer."

Then the disciples understood that Jesus was talking to them about John the Baptist.

When Jesus and those who were with him came to the other disciples, they saw a large crowd around them. The teachers of the law were arguing with them. When all the people saw Jesus, they were filled with wonder. And they ran to greet him.

"What are you arguing with them about?" Jesus asked.

A man in the crowd answered. "Teacher," he said. "I have brought you my son." He got on his knees in front of him. "Lord," he said, "have mercy on my son. He is my only child. He is controlled by a spirit. Because of this, my son can't speak anymore. He shakes wildly and suffers a great deal. A spirit takes hold of him, and he suddenly screams. It throws him into fits so that he foams at the mouth. He grinds his teeth. And his body becomes stiff. It hardly ever leaves him. It is destroying him. He often falls into the fire or into water. I brought him to your disciples. I begged your disciples to drive it out. But they couldn't do it."

"You unbelieving and evil people!" Jesus replied. "How long do I have to stay with you? How long do I have to put up with you? Bring the boy here to me."

So they brought him. As soon as the spirit saw Jesus, it threw the boy into a fit. He fell to the ground. He rolled around and foamed at the mouth.

Jesus asked the boy's father, "How long has he been like this?"

"Since he was a child," he answered. "The spirit has often thrown him into fire or water to kill him. But if you can do anything, please take pity on us. Please help us."

"'If you can'?" said Jesus. "Everything is possible for the one who believes."

Right away the boy's father cried out, "I do believe! Help me overcome my unbelief!"

Jesus saw that a crowd was running over to see what was happening. Then he ordered the evil spirit to leave the boy. "You spirit that makes him unable to hear and speak!" he said. "I command you, come out of him. Never enter him again."

The spirit screamed. It shook the boy wildly. Then it came out of him. The boy looked so lifeless that many people said, "He's dead." But Jesus took him by the hand. He lifted the boy to his feet, and the boy stood up. They were all amazed at God's greatness.

Jesus went indoors. Then his disciples asked him in private, "Why couldn't we drive out the evil spirit?"

He replied, "Because your faith is much too small. This kind can come out only by prayer. What I'm about to tell you is true. If you have faith as small as a mustard seed, it is enough. You can say to this mountain, 'Move from here to there.' And it will move. Nothing will be impossible for you."

They left that place and passed through Galilee. Jesus did not want anyone to know where they were. That was because he was teaching his disciples.

Everyone was wondering about all that Jesus did. Then Jesus said to his disciples, "Listen carefully to what I am about to tell you. The Son of Man is going to be handed over to men. They will kill him. On the third day he will rise from the dead." But they didn't understand what this meant. That was because it was hidden from them. And they were afraid to ask Jesus about it.

Jesus and his disciples arrived in Capernaum. There the tax collectors came to Peter. They asked him, "Doesn't your teacher pay the temple tax?"[3]

"Yes, he does," he replied.

When Peter came into the house, Jesus spoke first. "What do you think, Simon?" he asked. "Who do the kings of the earth collect taxes and fees from? Do they collect from their own sons or from others?"

"From others," Peter answered.

"Then the sons don't have to pay," Jesus said to him. "But we don't want to make them angry. So go to the lake and throw out your fishing line. Take the first fish you catch. Open its mouth. There you will find the exact coin you need. Take it and give it to them for my tax and yours."

Jesus and his disciples came to a house in Capernaum. There he asked them, "What were you arguing about on the road?" But they kept quiet. On the way, they had argued about which one of them was the most important person.

Jesus sat down and called for the Twelve to come to him.

Jesus knew what they were thinking. So he said, "If you want to be first, you must be the very last. You must be the servant of everyone."

Jesus took a little child and had the child stand among them. Then he took the child in his arms. Jesus said, "What I'm about to tell you is true. You need to change and become like little children. If you don't, you will never enter the kingdom of heaven. Anyone who becomes as free of pride as this child is the most important in the kingdom of heaven.

"Anyone who welcomes a little child like this in my name welcomes me. And anyone who welcomes me doesn't welcome only me but also the One who sent me. The least important person among all of you is the most important."

"Master," said John, "we saw a man driving out demons in your name. We tried to stop him, because he is not one of us."

"Do not stop him," Jesus said. "No one who does a miracle in my name can in the next moment say anything bad about me. Anyone who is not against us is for us.

"What I'm about to tell you is true. Suppose someone gives you a cup of water in my name because you belong to me. That one will certainly not go without a reward.

"But what if someone leads one of these little ones who believe in me to sin? If he does, it would be better for him to have a large millstone hung around his neck and be drowned at the bottom of the sea.

"How terrible it will be for the world because of the things that lead people to sin! Things like that must come. But how terrible for those who cause them!

"If your hand causes you to sin, cut it off. It would be better for you to enter God's kingdom with only one hand than to go into hell with two hands. In hell the fire never goes out.

"If your foot causes you to sin, cut it off. It would be better for you to enter God's kingdom with only one foot than to have two feet and be thrown into hell.

"If your eye causes you to sin, poke it out. It would be better for you to enter God's kingdom with only one eye than to have two eyes and be thrown into hell. In hell,

"'The worms do not die.

The fire is not put out.'[4]

Everyone will be salted with fire.

"Salt is good. But suppose it loses its saltiness. How can you make it salty again? Have salt in yourselves. And be at peace with each other.

"See that you don't look down on one of these little ones. Here is what I tell you. Their angels in heaven can go at any time to see my Father who is in heaven.

"What do you think? Suppose a man owns 100 sheep and one of them wanders away. Won't he leave the 99 sheep on the hills? Won't he go and look for the one that wandered off? What I'm about to tell you is true. If he finds that sheep, he is happier about the one than about the 99 that didn't wander off. It is the same with your Father in heaven. He does not want any of these little ones to be lost.

"If your brother sins against you, go to him. Tell him what he did wrong. Keep it between the two of you. If he listens to you, you have won him back.

"But what if he won't listen to you? Then take one or two others with you. Scripture says, 'Every matter must be proved by the words of two or three witnesses.'[5] But what if he also refuses to listen to the witnesses? Then tell it to the church. And what if he refuses to listen even to the church? Then don't treat him as your brother. Treat him as you would treat an ungodly person or a tax collector.

"What I'm about to tell you is true. What you lock on earth will be locked in heaven. What you unlock on earth will be unlocked in heaven.

"Again, here is what I tell you. Suppose two of you on earth agree about anything you ask for. My Father in heaven will do it for you. Where two or three people meet together in my name, I am there with them."

Peter came to Jesus. He asked, "Lord, how many times should I forgive my brother when he sins against me? Up to seven times?"

Jesus answered, "I tell you, not seven times, but 77 times.

"The kingdom of heaven is like a king who wanted to collect all the money his servants owed him. As the king began to do it, a man who owed him millions of dollars was brought to him. The man was not able to pay. So his master gave an order. The man, his wife, his children, and all he owned had to be sold to pay back what he owed.

"The servant fell on his knees in front of him. 'Give me time,' he begged. 'I'll pay everything back.'

"His master felt sorry for him. He forgave him what he owed and let him go.

"But then that servant went out and found one of the other servants who owed him a few dollars. He grabbed him and began to choke him. 'Pay back what you owe me!' he said.

"The other servant fell on his knees. 'Give me time,' he begged him. 'I'll pay you back.'

"But the first servant refused. Instead, he went and had the man thrown into prison. The man would be held there until he could pay back what he owed. The other servants saw what had happened. It troubled them greatly. They went and told their master everything that had happened.

"Then the master called the first servant in. 'You evil servant,' he said. 'I forgave all that you owed me because you begged me to. Shouldn't you have had mercy on the other servant just as I had mercy on you?' In anger his master turned him over to the jailers. He would be punished until he paid back everything he owed.

"This is how my Father in heaven will treat each of you unless you forgive your brother from your heart."

After this, Jesus went around in Galilee. He stayed away from Judea on purpose. He knew that the Jews there were waiting to kill him.

chapter eleven

Claiming God's Name

The Jewish Feast of Booths was near.[1] Jesus' brothers said to him, "You should leave here and go to Judea. Then your disciples will see the kinds of things you do. No one who wants to be well known does things in secret. Since you are doing these things, show yourself to the world."

Even Jesus' own brothers did not believe in him.

So Jesus told them, "The right time has not yet come for me. For you, any time is right. The people of the world can't hate you. But they hate me. This is because I give witness that what they do is evil.

"You go to the Feast. I am not yet going up to this Feast. For me, the right time has not yet come."

After he said this, he stayed in Galilee.

The time grew near for Jesus to be taken up to heaven. So he made up his mind to go to Jerusalem. When his brothers had left for the Feast, he went also. But he went secretly, not openly.

He sent messengers on ahead. They went into a Samaritan village to get things ready for him. But the people there did not welcome Jesus. That was because he was heading for Jerusalem.

The disciples James and John saw this. They asked, "Lord, do you want us to call down fire from heaven to destroy them?"

But Jesus turned and commanded them not to do it. They went on to another village.

Once Jesus and those who were with him were walking along the road. A man said to Jesus, "I will follow you no matter where you go."

Jesus replied, "Foxes have holes. Birds of the air have nests. But the Son of Man has no place to lay his head."

He said to another man, "Follow me." But the man replied, "Lord, first let me go and bury my father."

Jesus said to him, "Let dead people bury their own dead. You go and tell others about God's kingdom."

Still another man said, "I will follow you, Lord. But first let me go back and say good-by to my family."

Jesus replied, "Suppose you start to plow and then look back. If you do, you are not fit for service in God's kingdom."

At the Feast the Jews were watching for him. They were asking, "Where is he?"

Many people in the crowd were whispering about him. Some said, "He is a good man." Others replied, "No. He fools the people."

But no one would say anything about him openly. They were afraid of the Jews.

Jesus did nothing until halfway through the Feast. Then he went up to the temple courtyard and began to teach. The Jews were amazed. They asked, "How did this man learn so much without studying?"

Jesus answered, "What I teach is not my own. It comes from the One who sent me. Anyone who chooses to do what God wants him to do will find out whether my teaching comes from God or from me. Someone who speaks on his own does it to get honor for himself. But someone who works for the honor of the One who sent him is truthful. There is nothing false about him.

"Didn't Moses give you the law? But not one of you keeps the law. Why are you trying to kill me?"

"You are controlled by demons," the crowd answered. "Who is trying to kill you?"

Jesus said to them, "I did one miracle, and you are all amazed. Moses gave you circumcision, and so you circumcise a child on the Sabbath day. But circumcision did not really come from Moses. It came from Abraham. You circumcise a child on the Sabbath day. You think that if you do, you won't break the law of Moses. Then why are you angry with me? I healed a whole man on the Sabbath!

"Stop judging only by what you see. Judge correctly."

Then some of the people of Jerusalem began asking questions. They said, "Isn't this the man some people are trying to kill? Here he is! He is speaking openly. They aren't saying a word to him. Have the authorities really decided that he is the Christ? But we know where this man is from. When the Christ comes, no one will know where he is from."

Jesus was still teaching in the temple courtyard. He cried out, "Yes, you know me. And you know where I am from. I am not here on my own. The One who sent me is true. You do not know him. But I know him. I am from him, and he sent me."

When he said this, they tried to arrest him. But no one laid a hand on him. His time had not yet come.

Still, many people in the crowd put their faith in him. They said, "How will it be when the Christ comes? Will he do more miraculous signs than this man?"

The Pharisees heard the crowd whispering things like this about him. Then the chief priests and the Pharisees sent temple guards to arrest him.

Jesus said, "I am with you for only a short time. Then I will go to the One who sent me. You will look for me, but you won't find me. You can't come where I am going."

The Jews said to one another, "Where does this man plan to go? Does he think we can't find him? Will he go where our people live scattered among the Greeks? Will he go there to teach the Greeks?

What did he mean when he said, 'You will look for me, but you won't find me'? And, 'You can't come where I am going'?"

It was the last and most important day of the Feast. Jesus stood up and spoke in a loud voice. He said, "Let anyone who is thirsty come to me and drink. Does anyone believe in me? Then, just as Scripture says, streams of living water will flow from inside him."

When he said this, he meant the Holy Spirit. Those who believed in Jesus would receive the Spirit later. Up to that time, the Spirit had not been given. This was because Jesus had not yet received glory.

When some of the people heard his words, they said, "This man must be the Prophet we've been expecting."

Others said, "He is the Christ."

Still others asked, "How can the Christ come from Galilee? Doesn't Scripture say that the Christ will come from David's family? Doesn't it say that he will come from Bethlehem, the town where David lived?"[2]

So the people did not agree about who Jesus was. Some wanted to arrest him. But no one laid a hand on him.

Finally the temple guards went back to the chief priests and the Pharisees. They asked the guards, "Why didn't you bring him in?"

"No one ever spoke the way this man does," the guards replied.

"You mean he has fooled you also?" the Pharisees asked. "Have any of the rulers or Pharisees believed in him? No! But this mob knows nothing about the law. There is a curse on them."

Then Nicodemus, a Pharisee, spoke. He was the one who had gone to Jesus earlier. He asked, "Does our law find someone guilty without hearing him first? Doesn't it want to find out what he is doing?"

They replied, "Are you from Galilee too? Look into it. You will find that a prophet does not come out of Galilee."

Then each of them went home. But Jesus went to the Mount of Olives.

At sunrise he arrived in the temple courtyard again. All the people gathered around him there. He sat down to teach them.

The teachers of the law and the Pharisees brought in a woman. She had been caught in adultery. They made her stand in front of the group. They said to Jesus, "Teacher, this woman was caught having sex with a man who was not her husband. In the Law, Moses commanded us to kill such women by throwing stones at them.[3] Now what do you say?" They were trying to trap Jesus with that question. They wanted to have a reason to bring charges against him.

But Jesus bent down and started to write on the ground with his finger.

They kept asking him questions. So he stood up and said to them, "Has any one of you not sinned? Then you be the first to throw a stone at her."

He bent down again and wrote on the ground.

Those who heard what he had said began to go away. They left one at a time, the older ones first. Soon only Jesus was left. The woman was still standing there.

Jesus stood up and asked her, "Woman, where are they? Hasn't anyone found you guilty?"

"No one, sir," she said.

"Then I don't find you guilty either," Jesus said. "Go now and leave your life of sin."

Jesus spoke to the people again. He said, "I am the light of the world. Those who follow me will never walk in darkness. They will have the light that leads to life."

The Pharisees argued with him. "Here you are," they said, "appearing as your own witness. But your witness does not count."

Jesus answered, "Even if I give witness about myself, my witness does count. I know where I came from. And I know where I am going. But you have no idea where I come from or where I am going. You judge by human standards. I don't judge anyone.

"But if I do judge, what I decide is right. This is because I am not alone. I stand with the Father, who sent me. Your own Law says that the witness of two is what counts. I give witness about myself. My other witness is the Father, who sent me."

Then they asked him, "Where is your father?"[4]

"You do not know me or my Father," Jesus replied. "If you knew me, you would know my Father also."

He spoke these words while he was teaching in the temple area. He was near the place where the offerings were put. But no one arrested him. His time had not yet come.

Once more Jesus spoke to them. "I am going away," he said. "You will look for me, and you will die in your sin. You can't come where I am going."

This made the Jews ask, "Will he kill himself? Is that why he says, 'You can't come where I am going'?"

But Jesus said, "You are from below. I am from heaven. You are from this world. I am not from this world. I told you that you would die in your sins. Do you believe that I am the one I claim to be? If you don't, you will certainly die in your sins."

"Who are you?" they asked.

"Just what I have been claiming all along," Jesus replied. "I have a lot to say that will judge you. But the One who sent me can be trusted. And I tell the world what I have heard from him."

They did not understand that Jesus was telling them about his Father. So Jesus said, "You will lift up the Son of Man. Then you will know that I am the one I claim to be. You will also know that I do nothing on my own. I speak just what the Father has taught me. The One who sent me is with me. He has not left me alone, because I always do what pleases him."

Even while Jesus was speaking, many people put their faith in him.

Jesus spoke to the Jews who had believed him. "If you obey my teaching," he said, "you are really my disciples. Then you will know the truth. And the truth will set you free."

They answered him, "We are Abraham's children. We have never been slaves of anyone. So how can you say that we will be set free?"

Jesus replied, "What I'm about to tell you is true. Everyone who sins is a slave of sin. A slave has no lasting place in the family. But a son belongs to the family forever. So if the Son of Man sets you free, you will really be free.

"I know you are Abraham's children. But you are ready to kill me. You have no room for my word. I am telling you what I saw when I was with my Father. You do what you have heard from your father."

"Abraham is our father," they answered.

Jesus said, "Are you really Abraham's children? If you are, you will do the things Abraham did. But you have decided to kill me. I am a man who has told you the truth I heard from God. Abraham didn't do the things you want to do. You are doing the things your own father does."

"We are not children of people who weren't married to each other," they objected. "The only Father we have is God himself."

Jesus said to them, "If God were your Father, you would love me. I came from God, and now I am here. I have not come on my own. He sent me.

"Why aren't my words clear to you? Because you can't really hear what I say. You belong to your father, the devil. You want to obey your father's wishes.

"From the beginning, the devil was a murderer. He has never obeyed the truth. There is no truth in him. When he lies, he speaks his natural language. He does this because he is a liar. He is the father of lies.

"But because I tell the truth, you don't believe me! Can any of you prove I am guilty of sinning? Am I not telling the truth? Then why don't you believe me?

"Everyone who belongs to God hears what God says. The reason you don't hear is that you don't belong to God."

The Jews answered Jesus, "Aren't we right when we say you are a Samaritan? Aren't you controlled by a demon?"

"I am not controlled by a demon," said Jesus. "I honor my Father. You do not honor me. I am not seeking glory for myself. But there is One who brings glory to me. He is the judge. What I'm about to tell you is true. Anyone who obeys my word will never die."

Then the Jews cried out, "Now we know you are controlled by a demon! Abraham died. So did the prophets. But you say that anyone who obeys your word will never die. Are you greater than our father Abraham? He died. So did the prophets. Who do you think you are?"

Jesus replied, "If I bring glory to myself, my glory means nothing. You claim that my Father is your God. He is the one who brings glory to me. You do not know him. But I know him. If I said I did not, I would be a liar like you. But I do know him. And I obey his word.

"Your father Abraham was filled with joy at the thought of seeing my day. He saw it and was glad."

"You are not even 50 years old," the Jews said to Jesus. "And you have seen Abraham?"

"What I'm about to tell you is true," Jesus answered. "Before Abraham was born, I am!"[5]

When he said this, they picked up stones to kill him. But Jesus hid himself. He slipped away from the temple area.

chapter twelve

Who is He?

After this the Lord appointed 72 others. He sent them out two by two ahead of him. They went to every town and place where he was about to go.

He told them, "The harvest is huge, but the workers are few. So ask the Lord of the harvest to send out workers into his harvest field.

"Go! I am sending you out like lambs among wolves. Do not take a purse or bag or sandals. And don't greet anyone on the road.

"When you enter a house, first say, 'May this house be blessed with peace.' If someone there loves peace, your blessing of peace will rest on him. If not, it will return to you. Stay in that house. Eat and drink anything they give you. Workers are worthy of their pay. Do not move around from house to house.

"When you enter a town and are welcomed, eat what is set down in front of you. Heal the sick people who are there. Tell them, 'God's kingdom is near you.'

"But what if you enter a town and are not welcomed? Then go into its streets and say, 'We wipe off even the dust of your town that sticks to our feet. We do it to show that God isn't pleased with you. But here is what you can be sure of. God's kingdom is near.'"

Jesus began to speak against the cities where he had done most of his miracles. The people there had not turned away from their sins. So he said, "How terrible it will be for you, Korazin! How terrible for you, Bethsaida! Suppose the miracles done in you had been done in Tyre and Sidon. They would have turned away from their sins long ago. They would have put on black clothes. They would have sat down in ashes. But I tell you this. On judgment day it will be easier for Tyre and Sidon than for you. [1]

"And what about you, Capernaum? Will you be lifted up to heaven? No! You will go down to the place of the dead. Suppose the miracles done in you had been done in Sodom. It would still be here today. But I tell you this. On judgment day it will be easier for Sodom than for you.

"Anyone who listens to you listens to me. Anyone who does not accept you does not accept me. And anyone who does not accept me does not accept the One who sent me."

The 72 returned with joy. They said, "Lord, even the demons obey us when we speak in your name."

Jesus replied, "I saw Satan fall like lightning from heaven. I have given you authority to walk all over snakes and scorpions. You will be able to destroy all the power of the enemy. Nothing will harm you. But do not be glad when the evil spirits obey you. Instead, be glad that your names are written in heaven."

At that time Jesus was full of joy through the Holy Spirit. He said, "I praise you, Father. You are Lord of heaven and earth. You have hidden these things from the wise and educated. But you have shown them to little children. Yes, Father. This is what you wanted.

"My Father has given all things to me. The Father is the only one who knows who the Son is. And the only ones who know the Father are the Son and those to whom the Son chooses to make the Father known."

Then Jesus turned to his disciples. He said to them in private, "Blessed are the eyes that see what you see. I tell you, many prophets and kings wanted to see what you see. But they didn't see it. They wanted to hear what you hear. But they didn't hear it."

One day an authority on the law stood up to put Jesus to the test. "Teacher," he asked, "what must I do to receive eternal life?"

"What is written in the Law?" Jesus replied. "How do you understand it?"

He answered, "'Love the Lord your God with all your heart and with all your soul. Love him with all your strength and with all your mind.' And, 'Love your neighbor as you love yourself.'"[2]

"You have answered correctly," Jesus replied. "Do that, and you will live."

But the man wanted to make himself look good. So he asked Jesus, "And who is my neighbor?"

Jesus replied, "A man was going down from Jerusalem to Jericho. Robbers attacked him. They stripped off his clothes and beat him. Then they went away, leaving him almost dead. A priest happened to be going down that same road. When he saw the man, he passed by on the other side. A Levite also came by.[3] When he saw the man, he passed by on the other side too.

"But a Samaritan came to the place where the man was. When he saw the man, he felt sorry for him. He went to him, poured olive oil and wine on his wounds and ban-daged them. Then he put the man on his own donkey. He took him to an inn and took care of him. The next day he took out two silver coins. He gave them to the owner of the inn. 'Take care of him,' he said. 'When I return, I will pay you back for any extra expense you may have.'

"Which of the three do you think was a neighbor to the man who was attacked by robbers?"

The authority on the law replied, "The one who felt sorry for him."

Jesus told him, "Go and do as he did."

Jesus and his disciples went on their way. Jesus came to a village where a woman named Martha lived. She welcomed him into her home. She had a sister named Mary.

Mary sat at the Lord's feet listening to what he said. But Martha was busy with all the things that had to be done. She came to Jesus and said, "Lord, my sister has left me to do the work by myself. Don't you care? Tell her to help me!"

"Martha, Martha," the Lord answered. "You are worried and upset about many things. But only one thing is needed. Mary has chosen what is better. And it will not be taken away from her."

One day Jesus was praying in a certain place. When he finished, one of his disciples spoke to him. "Lord," he said, "teach us to pray, just as John taught his disciples."

Jesus said to them, "When you pray, this is what you should say:

"'Father, may your name be honored.

May your kingdom come.

Give us each day our daily bread.

Forgive us our sins,

as we also forgive everyone who sins against us.

Keep us from falling into sin when we are tempted.'"

Then Jesus said to them, "Suppose someone has a friend. He goes to him at midnight. He says, 'Friend, lend me three loaves of bread. A friend of mine on a journey has come to stay with me. I have nothing for him to eat.'

"Then the one inside answers, 'Don't bother me. The door is already locked. My children are with me in bed. I can't get up and give you anything.'

"I tell you, that person will not get up. And he won't give the man bread just because he is his friend. But because the man keeps on asking, he will get up. He will give him as much as he needs.

"So here is what I say to you. Ask, and it will be given to you. Search, and you will find. Knock, and the door will be opened to you. Everyone who asks will receive. He who searches will find. And the door will be opened to the one who knocks.

"Fathers, suppose your son asks for a fish. Which of you will give him a snake instead? Or suppose he asks for an egg. Which of you will give him a scorpion? Even though you are evil, you know how to give good gifts to your children. How much more will your Father who is in heaven give the Holy Spirit to those who ask him!"

Jesus finished speaking. Then a Pharisee invited him to eat with him. So Jesus went in and took his place at the table. But the Pharisee noticed that Jesus did not wash before the meal. He was surprised.

Then the Lord spoke to him. "You Pharisees clean the outside of the cup and dish," he said. "But inside you are full of greed and evil. You foolish people! Didn't the one who made the outside make the inside also? Give to poor people what is inside the dish. Then everything will be clean for you. Blind Pharisee! First clean the inside of the cup and dish. Then the outside will also be clean.

"How terrible it will be for you, teachers of the law and Pharisees! You pretenders! You shut the kingdom of heaven in people's faces. You yourselves do not enter. And you will not let those enter who are trying to.

"How terrible for you, teachers of the law and Pharisees! You pretenders! You travel everywhere to win one person to your faith. Then you make him twice as much a son of hell as you are.

"How terrible for you, blind guides! You say, 'If anyone takes an oath in the name of the temple, it means nothing. But anyone who takes an oath in the name of the gold of the temple must keep the oath.' You are blind and foolish! Which is more important? Is it the gold? Or is it the temple that makes the gold holy?

"You also say, 'If anyone takes an oath in the name of the altar, it means nothing. But anyone who takes an oath in the name of the gift on it must keep the oath.' You blind men! Which is more important? Is it the gift? Or is it the altar that makes the gift holy?

"So anyone who takes an oath in the name of the altar takes an oath in the name of it and of everything on it. And anyone who takes an oath in the name of the temple takes an oath in the name of it and of the One who lives in it. And anyone who takes an oath in the name of heaven takes an oath in the name of God's throne and of the One who sits on it.

"How terrible it will be for you teachers of the law and Pharisees! You pretenders! You give God a tenth of your spices, like mint, dill and cummin. But you have not practiced the more important things of the law, like fairness, mercy and faithfulness. You should have practiced the last things without failing to do the first. You blind guides! You remove the smallest insect from your food. But you swallow a whole camel!

"How terrible for you, teachers of the law and Pharisees! You pretenders! You are like tombs that are painted white. They look beautiful on the outside. But on the inside they are full of the bones of the dead. They are also full of other things that are not pure and clean. It is the same with you. On the outside you seem to be doing what is right. But on the inside you are full of what is wrong. You pretend to be what you are not.

"How terrible for you, teachers of the law and Pharisees! You pretenders! You build tombs for the prophets. You decorate the graves of the godly. And you say, 'If we had lived in the days of those who lived before us, we wouldn't have done what they did. We wouldn't have helped to kill the prophets.' So you give witness against yourselves. You admit that you are the children of those who murdered the prophets. So finish the sins that those who lived before you started!

"You nest of poisonous snakes! How will you escape from being sentenced to hell? God in his wisdom said, 'I will send prophets and apostles to them. They will kill some. And they will try to hurt others.' So the people of today will be punished. They will pay for all the prophets' blood spilled since the world began. I mean from the blood of Abel to the blood of Zechariah, who was killed between the altar and the temple.[4] Yes, I tell you, the people of today will be punished for all these things.

"How terrible for you authorities on the law! You have taken away the key to the door of knowledge. You yourselves have not entered. And you have stood in the way of those who were entering."

When Jesus left there, the Pharisees and the teachers of the law strongly opposed him. They threw a lot of questions at him. They set traps for him. They wanted to catch him in something he might say.

During that time a crowd of many thousands had gathered. There were so many people that they were stepping on one another.

Jesus spoke first to his disciples. "Be on your guard against the yeast of the Pharisees," he said. "They just pretend to be godly."

Someone in the crowd spoke to Jesus. "Teacher," he said, "tell my brother to divide the family property with me."

Jesus replied, "Friend, who made me a judge or umpire between you?"

Then he said to them, "Watch out! Be on your guard against wanting to have more and more things. Life is not made up of how much a person has."

Then Jesus told them a story. He said, "A certain rich man's land produced a good crop. He thought to himself, 'What should I do? I don't have anyplace to store my crops.'

"Then he said, 'This is what I'll do. I will tear down my storerooms and build bigger ones. I will store all my grain and my other things in them. I'll say to myself, "You have plenty of good things stored away for many years. Take life easy. Eat, drink and have a good time."'

"But God said to him, 'You foolish man! This very night I will take your life away from you. Then who will get what you have prepared for yourself?'

"That is how it will be for anyone who stores things away for himself but is not rich in God's eyes."

Jesus spoke to the crowd. He said, "You see a cloud rising in the west. Right away you say, 'It's going to rain.' And it does. The south wind blows. So you say, 'It's going to be hot.' And it is. You pretenders! You know how to understand the appearance of the earth and the sky. Why can't you understand the meaning of what is happening right now?

"Why don't you judge for yourselves what is right?"

Some people who were there at that time told Jesus about certain Galileans. Pilate had mixed their blood with their sacrifices.[5]

Jesus said, "These people from Galilee suffered greatly. Do you think they were worse sinners than all the other Galileans? I tell you, no! But unless you turn away from your sins, you will all die too. Or what about the 18 people in Siloam? They died when the tower fell on them. Do you think they were more guilty than all the others living in Jerusalem? I tell you, no! But unless you turn away from your sins, you will all die too."

Then Jesus told a story. "A man had a fig tree," he said. "It had been planted in his vineyard. When he went to look for fruit on it, he didn't find any. So he went to the man who took care of the vineyard. He said, 'For three years now I've been coming to look for fruit on this fig tree. But I haven't found any. Cut it down! Why should it use up the soil?'

"'Sir,' the man replied, 'leave it alone for one more year. I'll dig around it and feed it. If it bears fruit next year, fine! If not, then cut it down.'"

Jesus was teaching in one of the synagogues on a Sabbath day. A woman there had been disabled by an evil spirit for 18 years. She was bent over and could not stand up straight.

Jesus saw her. He asked her to come to him. He said to her, "Woman, you will no longer be disabled. I am about to set you free." Then he put his hands on her.

Right away she stood up straight and praised God.

Jesus had healed the woman on the Sabbath day. This made the synagogue ruler angry. He told the people, "There are six days for work. So come and be healed on those days. But do not come on the Sabbath."

The Lord answered him, "You pretenders! Doesn't each of you go to the barn and untie his ox or donkey on the Sabbath day? Then don't you lead it out to give it water? This woman is a member of

Abraham's family line. But Satan has kept her disabled for 18 long years. Shouldn't she be set free on the Sabbath day from what was keeping her disabled?"

When Jesus said this, all those who opposed him were put to shame. But the people were delighted. They loved all the wonderful things he was doing.

As Jesus went along, he saw a man who was blind. He had been blind since he was born. Jesus' disciples asked him, "Rabbi, who sinned? Was this man born blind because he sinned? Or did his parents sin?"[6]

"It isn't because this man sinned," said Jesus. "It isn't because his parents sinned. This happened so that God's work could be shown in his life. While it is still day, we must do the work of the One who sent me. Night is coming. Then no one can work. While I am in the world, I am the light of the world."

After he said this, he spit on the ground. He made some mud with the spit. Then he put the mud on the man's eyes.

"Go," he told him. "Wash in the Pool of Siloam." Siloam means Sent.

So the man went and washed. And he came home able to see.

His neighbors and those who had earlier seen him begging asked questions. "Isn't this the same man who used to sit and beg?" they asked.

Some claimed that he was.

Others said, "No. He only looks like him."

But the man who had been blind kept saying, "I am the man."

"Then how were your eyes opened?" they asked.

He replied, "The man they call Jesus made some mud and put it on my eyes. He told me to go to Siloam and wash. So I went and washed. Then I could see."

"Where is this man?" they asked him.

"I don't know," he said.

They brought to the Pharisees the man who had been blind. The day Jesus made the mud and opened the man's eyes was a Sabbath. So the Pharisees also asked him how he was able to see.

"He put mud on my eyes," the man replied. "Then I washed. And now I can see."

Some of the Pharisees said, "Jesus has not come from God. He does not keep the Sabbath day."

But others asked, "How can a sinner do such miraculous signs?"

So the Pharisees did not agree with each other.

Finally they turned again to the blind man. "What do you have to say about him?" they asked. "It was your eyes he opened."

The man replied, "He is a prophet."

The Jews still did not believe that the man had been blind and now could see. So they sent for his parents. "Is this your son?" they asked. "Is this the one you say was born blind? How is it that now he can see?"

"We know he is our son," the parents answered. "And we know he was born blind. But we don't know how he can now see. And we don't know who opened his eyes. Ask him. He is an adult. He can speak for himself."

His parents said this because they were afraid of the Jews. The Jews had already decided that anyone who said Jesus was the Christ would be put out of the synagogue. That was why the man's parents said, "He is an adult. Ask him."

Again they called the man who had been blind to come to them. "Give glory to God by telling the truth!" they said. "We know that the man who healed you is a sinner."

He replied, "I don't know if he is a sinner or not. I do know one thing. I was blind, but now I can see!"

Then they asked him, "What did he do to you? How did he open your eyes?"

He answered, "I have already told you. But you didn't listen. Why do you want to hear it again? Do you want to become his disciples too?"

Then they began to attack him with their words. "You are this fellow's disciple!" they said. "We are disciples of Moses! We know that God spoke to Moses. But we don't even know where this fellow comes from."

The man answered, "That is really surprising! You don't know where he comes from, and yet he opened my eyes. We know that God does not listen to sinners. He listens to godly people who do what he wants them to do. Nobody has ever heard of anyone opening the eyes of a person born blind. If this man had not come from God, he could do nothing."

Then the Pharisees replied, "When you were born, you were already deep in sin. How dare you talk like that to us!" And they threw him out of the synagogue.

Jesus heard that the Pharisees had thrown the man out. When he found him, he said, "Do you believe in the Son of Man?"

"Who is he, sir?" the man asked. "Tell me, so I can believe in him."

Jesus said, "You have now seen him. In fact, he is the one speaking with you."

Then the man said, "Lord, I believe." And he worshiped him.

Jesus said, "I have come into this world to judge it. I have come so that the blind will see and those who see will become blind."

Some Pharisees who were with him heard him say this. They asked, "What? Are we blind too?"

Jesus said, "If you were blind, you would not be guilty of sin. But since you claim you can see, you remain guilty.

"What I'm about to tell you is true. What if someone does not enter the sheep pen through the gate but climbs in another way? That person is a thief and a robber. The one who enters through the gate is the shepherd of the sheep. The gatekeeper opens the gate for him. The sheep listen to his voice. He calls his own sheep by name and leads them out. When he has brought all of his own sheep out, he goes on ahead of them. His sheep follow him because they know his voice. But they will never follow a stranger. In fact, they will run away from him. They don't recognize a stranger's voice."[7]

Jesus used this story. But the Jews who were there didn't understand what he was telling them.

So Jesus said again, "What I'm about to tell you is true. I am like a gate for the sheep. All those who ever came before me were thieves and robbers. But the sheep did not listen to them. I'm like a gate. Anyone who enters through me will be saved. He will come in and go out. And he will find plenty of food. The thief comes only to steal and kill and destroy. I have come so they can have life. I want them to have it in the fullest possible way.

"I am the good shepherd. The good shepherd gives his life for the sheep. The hired man is not the shepherd who owns the sheep. So when the hired man sees the wolf coming, he leaves the sheep and runs away. Then the wolf attacks the flock and scatters it. The man runs away because he is a hired man. He does not care about the sheep.

"I am the good shepherd. I know my sheep, and my sheep know me. They know me just as the Father knows me and I know the Father. And I give my life for the sheep.

"I have other sheep that do not belong to this sheep pen. I must bring them in too. They also will listen to my voice. Then there will be one flock and one shepherd.

"The reason my Father loves me is that I give up my life. But I will take it back again. No one takes it from me. I give it up myself. I have the authority to give it up. And I have the authority to take it back again. I received this command from my Father."

After Jesus spoke these words, the Jews again could not agree with each other. Many of them said, "He is controlled by a demon. He has gone crazy! Why should we listen to him?"

But others said, "A person controlled by a demon does not say things like this. Can a demon open the eyes of someone who is blind?"

Then came the Feast of Hanukkah[8] at Jerusalem. It was winter. Jesus was in the temple area walking in Solomon's Porch. The Jews gathered around him. They said, "How long will you keep us waiting? If you are the Christ, tell us plainly."

Jesus answered, "I did tell you. But you do not believe. The kinds of things I do in my Father's name speak for me. But you do not believe, because you are not my sheep.

"My sheep listen to my voice. I know them, and they follow me. I give them eternal life, and they will never die. No one can steal them out of my hand. My Father, who has given them to me, is greater than anyone. No one can steal them out of my Father's hand. I and the Father are one."

Again the Jews picked up stones to kill him.

But Jesus said to them, "I have shown you many miracles from the Father. Which one of these are you throwing stones at me for?"

"We are not throwing stones at you for any of these," replied the Jews. "We are stoning you for saying a very evil thing.[9] You are only a man. But you claim to be God."

Jesus answered them, "Didn't God say in your Law, 'I have said you are gods'?[10] We know that Scripture is always true. God spoke to some people and called them 'gods.' If that is true, what about the One the Father set apart as his very own and sent into the world? Why do you charge me with saying a very evil thing? Is it because I said, 'I am God's Son'?

"Don't believe me unless I do what my Father does. But what if I do it? Even if you don't believe me, believe the miracles. Then you will know and understand that the Father is in me and I am in the Father."

Again they tried to arrest him. But he escaped from them.

Then Jesus went back across the Jordan River. He went to the place where John had been baptizing in the early days. There he stayed. Many people came to him. They said, "John never did a miraculous sign. But everything he said about this man was true." And in that place many believed in Jesus.

chapter thirteen

Raising the Dead

Then Jesus went through the towns and villages, teaching the people. He was on his way to Jerusalem. Someone asked him, "Lord, are only a few people going to be saved?"

He said to them, "Try very hard to enter through the narrow door. I tell you, many will try to enter and will not be able to. The owner of the house will get up and close the door. Then you will stand outside knocking and begging. You will say, 'Sir, open the door for us.'

"But he will answer, 'I don't know you. And I don't know where you come from.'

"Then you will say, 'We ate and drank with you. You taught in our streets.'

"But he will reply, 'I don't know you. And I don't know where you come from. Get away from me, all you who do evil!'

"You will sob and grind your teeth when you see those who are in God's kingdom. You will see Abraham, Isaac and Jacob[1] and all the prophets there. But you yourselves will be thrown out.

"People will come from east and west and north and south. They will take their places at the feast in God's kingdom. But those who think they belong to the kingdom will be thrown outside, into the darkness. There they will sob and grind their teeth. Then the last will be first. And the first will be last."

At that time some Pharisees came to Jesus. They said to him, "Leave this place. Go somewhere else. Herod wants to kill you."

He replied, "Go and tell that fox, 'I will drive out demons. I will heal people today and tomorrow. And on the third day I will reach my goal.' In any case, I must keep going today and tomorrow and the next day. Certainly no prophet can die outside Jerusalem!

"Jerusalem! Jerusalem! You kill the prophets and throw stones in order to kill those who are sent to you. Many times I have wanted to gather your people together. I have wanted to be like a hen who gathers her chicks under her wings. But you would not let me!

"Look, your house is left empty. I tell you, you will not see me again until you say, 'Blessed is the one who comes in the name of the Lord.'"[2]

One Sabbath day, Jesus went to eat in the house of a well-known Pharisee. While he was there, he was being carefully watched. In front of him was a man whose body was badly swollen.

Jesus turned to the Pharisees and the authorities on the law. He asked them, "Is it breaking the Law to heal on the Sabbath?"

But they remained silent.

So Jesus took hold of the man and healed him. Then he sent him away.

He asked them another question. He said, "Suppose one of you has a son or an ox that falls into a well on the Sabbath day. Wouldn't you pull him out right away?" And they had nothing to say.

Jesus noticed how the guests picked the places of honor at the table. So he told them a story. He said, "Suppose someone invites you to a wedding feast. Do not take the place of honor. A person more important than you may have been invited. If so, the host who invited both of you will come to you. He will say, 'Give this person your seat.' Then you will be filled with shame. You will have to take the least important place.

"But when you are invited, take the lowest place. Then your host will come over to you. He will say, 'Friend, move up to a better place.' Then you will be honored in front of all the other guests.

Anyone who lifts himself up will be brought down. And anyone who is brought down will be lifted up."

Then Jesus spoke to his host. "Suppose you give a lunch or a dinner," he said. "Do not invite your friends, your brothers or sisters, or your relatives, or your rich neighbors. If you do, they may invite you to eat with them. So you will be paid back.

"But when you give a big dinner, invite those who are poor. Also invite those who can't walk, the disabled and the blind. Then you will be blessed. Your guests can't pay you back. But you will be paid back when those who are right with God rise from the dead."

One of the people at the table with Jesus heard him say those things. So he said to Jesus, "Blessed is the one who will eat at the feast in God's kingdom."

Jesus replied, "A certain man was preparing a big dinner. He invited many guests. Then the day of the dinner arrived. He sent his servant to those who had been invited. The servant told them, 'Come. Everything is ready now.'

"But they all had the same idea. They began to make excuses. The first one said, 'I have just bought a field. I have to go and see it. Please excuse me.'

"Another said, 'I have just bought five pairs of oxen. I'm on my way to try them out. Please excuse me.'

"Still another said, 'I just got married, so I can't come.'

"The servant came back and reported this to his master.

"Then the owner of the house became angry. He ordered his servant, 'Go out quickly into the streets and lanes of the town. Bring in those who are poor. Also bring those who can't walk, the blind and the disabled.'

"'Sir,' the servant said, 'what you ordered has been done. But there is still room.'

"Then the master told his servant, 'Go out to the roads. Go out to the country lanes. Make the people come in. I want my house to be full. I tell you, not one of those men who were invited will get a taste of my dinner.'"

Large crowds were traveling with Jesus. He turned and spoke to them. He said, "Anyone who comes to me must hate his father and mother. He must hate his wife and children. He must hate his brothers and sisters. And he must hate even his own life. Unless he does, he can't be my disciple. Anyone who doesn't carry his cross and follow me can't be my disciple.

"Suppose someone wants to build a tower. Won't he sit down first and figure out how much it will cost? Then he will see whether he has enough money to finish it. Suppose he starts building and is not able to finish. Then everyone who sees what he has done will laugh at him. They will say, 'This fellow started to build. But he wasn't able to finish.'

"Or suppose a king is about to go to war against another king. And suppose he has 10,000 men, while the other has 20,000 coming against him. Won't he first sit down and think about whether he can win?

"And suppose he decides he can't win. Then he will send some men to ask how peace can be made. He will do this while the other king is still far away.

"In the same way, you must give up everything you have. If you don't, you can't be my disciple.

"Salt is good. But suppose it loses its saltiness. How can it be made salty again? It is not good for the soil. And it is not good for the trash pile. It will be thrown out.

"Those who have ears should listen."

The tax collectors and "sinners" were all gathering around to hear Jesus. But the Pharisees and the teachers of the law were whispering among themselves. They said, "This man welcomes sinners and eats with them."

Then Jesus told them a story. He said, "Suppose one of you has 100 sheep and loses one of them. Won't he leave the 99 in the open country? Won't he go and look for the one lost sheep until he finds it? When he finds it, he will joyfully put it on his shoulders and go home. Then he will call his friends and neighbors together. He will say, 'Be joyful with me. I have found my lost sheep.'

"I tell you, it will be the same in heaven. There will be great joy when one sinner turns away from sin. Yes, there will be more joy than for 99 godly people who do not need to turn away from their sins.

"Or suppose a woman has ten silver coins and loses one. She will light a lamp and sweep the house. She will search carefully until she finds the coin. And when she finds it, she will call her friends and neighbors together. She will say, 'Be joyful with me. I have found my lost coin.'

"I tell you, it is the same in heaven. There is joy in heaven over one sinner who turns away from sin."

Jesus continued, "There was a man who had two sons. The younger son spoke to his father. He said, 'Father, give me my share of the family property.' So the father divided his property between his two sons.

"Not long after that, the younger son packed up all he had. Then he left for a country far away. There he wasted his money on wild living. He spent everything he had.

"Then the whole country ran low on food. So the son didn't have what he needed. He went to work for someone who lived in that country, who sent him to the fields to feed the pigs. The son wanted to fill his stomach with the food the pigs were eating. But no one gave him anything.

"Then he began to think clearly again. He said, 'How many of my father's hired workers have more than enough food! But here I am dying from hunger! I will get up and go back to my father. I will say to him, "Father, I have sinned against heaven. And I have sinned against you. I am no longer fit to be called your son. Make me like one of your hired workers."' So he got up and went to his father.

"While the son was still a long way off, his father saw him. He was filled with tender love for his son. He ran to him. He threw his arms around him and kissed him.

"The son said to him, 'Father, I have sinned against heaven and against you. I am no longer fit to be called your son.'

"But the father said to his servants, 'Quick! Bring the best robe and put it on him. Put a ring on his finger and sandals on his feet. Bring the fattest calf and kill it. Let's have a big dinner and celebrate. This son of mine was dead. And now he is alive again. He was lost. And now he is found.'

"So they began to celebrate.

"The older son was in the field. When he came near the house, he heard music and dancing. So he called one of the servants. He asked him what was going on.

"'Your brother has come home,' the servant replied. 'Your father has killed the fattest calf. He has done this because your brother is back safe and sound.'

"The older brother became angry. He refused to go in. So his father went out and begged him.

"But he answered his father, 'Look! All these years I've worked like a slave for you. I have always obeyed your orders. You never gave me even a young goat so I could celebrate with my friends. But this son of yours wasted your money with some prostitutes. Now he comes home. And for him you kill the fattest calf!'

"'My son,' the father said, 'you are always with me. Everything I have is yours. But we had to celebrate and be glad. This brother of yours was dead. And now he is alive again. He was lost. And now he is found.'"

Jesus told his disciples another story. He said, "There was a rich man who had a manager. Some said that the manager was wasting what the rich man owned. So the rich man told him to come in. He asked him, 'What is this I hear about you? Tell me exactly how you have handled what I own. You can't be my manager any longer.'

"The manager said to himself, 'What will I do now? My master is taking away my job. I'm not strong enough to dig. And I'm too ashamed to beg. I know what I'm going to do. I'll do something so that when I lose my job here, people will welcome me into their houses.'

"So he called in each person who owed his master something. He asked the first one, 'How much do you owe my master?'

"'I owe 800 gallons of olive oil,' he replied.

"The manager told him, 'Take your bill. Sit down quickly and change it to 400 gallons.'

"Then he asked the second one, 'And how much do you owe?'

"'I owe 1,000 bushels of wheat,' he replied.

"The manager told him, 'Take your bill and change it to 800 bushels.'

"The manager had not been honest. But the master praised him for being clever. The people of this world are clever in dealing with those who are like themselves. They are more clever than God's people.

"I tell you, use the riches of this world to help others. In that way, you will make friends for yourselves. Then when your riches are gone, you will be welcomed into your eternal home in heaven.

"Suppose you can be trusted with very little. Then you can be trusted with a lot. But suppose you are not honest with very little. Then you will not be honest with a lot.

"Suppose you have not been worthy of trust in handling worldly wealth. Then who will trust you with true riches? Suppose you have not been worthy of trust in handling someone else's property. Then who will give you property of your own?

"No servant can serve two masters at the same time. He will hate one of them and love the other. Or he will be faithful to one and dislike the other. You can't serve God and Money at the same time."

The Pharisees loved money. They heard all that Jesus said and made fun of him. Jesus said to them, "You try to make yourselves look good in the eyes of other people. But God knows your hearts. What is worth a great deal among people is hated by God.

"Once there was a rich man. He was dressed in purple cloth and fine linen. He lived an easy life every day. A man named Lazarus was placed at his gate. Lazarus was a beggar. His body was covered with sores. Even dogs came and licked his sores. All he wanted was to eat what fell from the rich man's table.

"The time came when the beggar died. The angels carried him to Abraham's side. The rich man also died and was buried. In hell, the rich man was suffering terribly. He looked up and saw Abraham far away. Lazarus was by his side. So the rich man called out, 'Father Abraham! Have pity on me! Send Lazarus to dip the tip of his finger in water. Then he can cool my tongue with it. I am in terrible pain in this fire.'

"But Abraham replied, 'Son, remember what happened in your lifetime. You received your good things. Lazarus received bad things. Now he is comforted here, and you are in terrible pain. Besides, a wide space has been placed between us and you. So those who want to go from here to you can't go. And no one can cross over from there to us.'

"The rich man answered, 'Then I beg you, father. Send Lazarus to my family. I have five brothers. Let Lazarus warn them. Then they will not come to this place of terrible suffering.'

"Abraham replied, 'They have the teachings of Moses and the Prophets. Let your brothers listen to them.'

"'No, father Abraham,' he said. 'But if someone from the dead goes to them, they will turn away from their sins.'

"Abraham said to him, 'They do not listen to Moses and the Prophets. So they will not be convinced even if someone rises from the dead.'"

Jesus spoke to his disciples. "Things that make people sin are sure to come," he said. "But how terrible it will be for the person who brings them! Suppose people lead one of these little ones to sin. It would be better for those people to be thrown into the sea with a millstone tied around their neck. So watch what you do.

"If your brother sins, tell him he is wrong. Then if he turns away from his sins, forgive him. Suppose he sins against you seven times in one day. And suppose he comes back to you each time and says, 'I'm sorry.' Forgive him."

The apostles said to the Lord, "Give us more faith!"

He replied, "Suppose you have faith as small as a mustard seed. Then you can say to this mulberry tree, 'Be pulled up. Be planted in the sea.' And it will obey you.

"Suppose one of you had a servant plowing or looking after the sheep. And suppose the servant came in from the field. Would you say to him, 'Come along now and sit down to eat'? No. Instead, you would say, 'Prepare my supper. Get yourself ready. Wait on me while I eat and drink. Then after that you can eat and drink.' Would you thank the servant because he did what he was told to do?

"It's the same with you. Suppose you have done everything you were told to do. Then you should say, 'We are not worthy to serve you. We have only done our duty.'"

A man named Lazarus[3] was sick. He was from Bethany, the village where Mary and her sister Martha lived. Mary would later pour perfume on the Lord. She would also wipe his feet with her hair. Her brother Lazarus was sick in bed. So the sisters sent a message to Jesus. "Lord," they told him, "the one you love is sick."

When Jesus heard this, he said, "This sickness will not end in death. No, it is for God's glory. God's Son will receive glory because of it."

Jesus loved Martha and her sister and Lazarus. But after he heard Lazarus was sick, he stayed where he was for two more days.

Then he said to his disciples, "Let us go back to Judea."

"But Rabbi," they said, "a short time ago the Jews tried to kill you with stones. Are you still going back there?"

Jesus answered, "Aren't there 12 hours of daylight? A person who walks during the day won't trip and fall. He can see because of this world's light. But when he walks at night, he'll trip and fall. He has no light."

After he said this, Jesus went on speaking to them. "Our friend Lazarus has fallen asleep," he said. "But I am going there to wake him up."

His disciples replied, "Lord, if he's sleeping, he will get better."

Jesus had been speaking about the death of Lazarus. But his disciples thought he meant natural sleep.

So then he told them plainly, "Lazarus is dead. For your benefit, I am glad I was not there. Now you will believe. But let us go to him."

Then Thomas, who was called Didymus, spoke to the rest of the disciples. "Let us go also," he said. "Then we can die with Jesus."

When Jesus arrived, he found out that Lazarus had already been in the tomb for four days. Bethany was less than two miles from Jerusalem. Many Jews had come to Martha and Mary. They had come to comfort them because their brother was dead.

When Martha heard that Jesus was coming, she went out to meet him. But Mary stayed at home.

"Lord," Martha said to Jesus, "I wish you had been here! Then my brother would not have died. But I know that even now God will give you anything you ask for."

Jesus said to her, "Your brother will rise again."

Martha answered, "I know he will rise again. This will happen when people are raised from the dead on the last day."

Jesus said to her, "I am the resurrection and the life. Anyone who believes in me will live, even if he dies. And those who live and believe in me will never die. Do you believe this?"

"Yes, Lord," she told him. "I believe that you are the Christ, the Son of God. I believe that you are the One who was supposed to come into the world."

After she said this, she went back home. She called her sister Mary to one side to talk to her. "The Teacher is here," Martha said. "He is asking for you."

When Mary heard this, she got up quickly and went to him.

Jesus had not yet entered the village. He was still at the place where Martha had met him. Some Jews had been comforting Mary in the house. They noticed how quickly she got up and went out. So they followed her. They thought she was going to the tomb to cry there.

Mary reached the place where Jesus was. When she saw him, she fell at his feet. She said, "Lord, I wish you had been here! Then my brother would not have died."

Jesus saw her crying. He saw that the Jews who had come along with her were crying also. His spirit became very sad, and he was troubled.

"Where have you put him?" he asked.

"Come and see, Lord," they replied.

Jesus sobbed.

Then the Jews said, "See how much he loved him!"

But some of them said, "He opened the eyes of the blind man. Couldn't he have kept this man from dying?"

Once more Jesus felt very sad. He came to the tomb. It was a cave with a stone in front of the entrance.

"Take away the stone," he said.

"But, Lord," said Martha, the sister of the dead man, "by this time there is a bad smell. Lazarus has been in the tomb for four days."

Then Jesus said, "Didn't I tell you that if you believed, you would see God's glory?"

So they took away the stone.

Then Jesus looked up. He said, "Father, I thank you for hearing me. I know that you always hear me. But I said this for the benefit of the people standing here. I said it so they will believe that you sent me."

Then Jesus called in a loud voice. He said, "Lazarus, come out!"

The dead man came out. His hands and feet were wrapped with strips of linen. A cloth was around his face.

Jesus said to them, "Take off the clothes he was buried in and let him go."

Many of the Jews who had come to visit Mary saw what Jesus did. So they put their faith in him.

But some of them went to the Pharisees. They told the Pharisees what Jesus had done. Then the chief priests and the Pharisees called a meeting of the Sanhedrin.[4]

"What can we do?" they asked. "This man is doing many miraculous signs. If we let him keep on doing this, everyone will believe in him. Then the Romans will come. They will take away our temple and our nation."[5]

One of them spoke up. His name was Caiaphas. He was high priest at that time. He said, "You don't know anything at all! You don't realize what is good for you. It is better if one man dies for the people than if the whole nation is destroyed."

He did not say this on his own. But he was high priest at that time. So he told ahead of time that Jesus would die for the Jewish nation. He also prophesied that Jesus would die for God's children scattered everywhere. He would die to bring them together and make them one.

So from that day on, the Jewish rulers planned to kill Jesus.

Jesus no longer moved around openly among the Jews. Instead, he went away to an area near the desert. He went to a village called Ephraim. There he stayed with his disciples.

chapter fourteen

Welcomed as King

It was almost time for the Jewish Passover Feast. Many people went up from the country to Jerusalem. They went there for the special washing that would make them pure before the Passover Feast. They kept looking for Jesus as they stood in the temple area. They asked one another, "What do you think? Isn't he coming to the Feast at all?"

But the chief priests and the Pharisees had given orders. They had commanded anyone who found out where Jesus was staying to report it. Then they could arrest him.

Jesus was on his way to Jerusalem. He traveled along the border between Samaria and Galilee. As he was going into a village, ten men met him. They had a skin disease. They were standing close by. And they called out in a loud voice, "Jesus! Master! Have pity on us!"

Jesus saw them and said, "Go. Show yourselves to the priests." While they were on the way, they were healed.

When one of them saw that he was healed, he came back. He praised God in a loud voice. He threw himself at Jesus' feet and thanked him. The man was a Samaritan.

Jesus asked, "Weren't all ten healed? Where are the other nine? Didn't anyone else return and give praise to God except this outsider?"

Then Jesus said to him, "Get up and go. Your faith has healed you."

Once the Pharisees asked Jesus when God's kingdom would come. He replied, "The coming of God's kingdom is not something you can see just by watching for it carefully. People will not say, 'Here it is.' Or, 'There it is.' God's kingdom is among you."

Then Jesus spoke to his disciples. "The time is coming," he said, "when you will long to see one of the days of the Son of Man. But you won't see it. People will tell you, 'There he is!' Or, 'Here he is!' Don't go running off after them.

"When the Son of Man comes, he will be like the lightning. It flashes and lights up the sky from one end to the other. But first the Son of Man must suffer many things. He will not be accepted by the people of today.

"Remember how it was in the days of Noah.[1] It will be the same when the Son of Man comes. People were eating and drinking. They were getting married. They were giving their daughters to be married. They did all those things right up to the day Noah entered the ark. Then the flood came and destroyed them all.

"It was the same in the days of Lot.[2] People were eating and drinking. They were buying and selling. They were planting and building. But on the day Lot left Sodom, fire and sulfur rained down from heaven. And all the people were destroyed.

"It will be just like that on the day the Son of Man is shown to the world. Suppose someone is on the roof of his house on that day. And suppose his goods are inside the house. He should not go down to get them. No one in the field should go back for anything either. Remember Lot's wife! Anyone who tries to keep his life will lose it. Anyone who loses his life will keep it.

"I tell you, on that night two people will be in one bed. One person will be taken and the other left. Two women will be grinding grain together. One will be taken and the other left."

"Where, Lord?" his disciples asked.

He replied, "The vultures will gather where there is a dead body."

Jesus told his disciples a story. He wanted to show them that they should always pray and not give up. He said, "In a certain town there was a judge. He didn't have any respect for God or care about people. A widow lived in that town. She came to the judge again and again. She kept begging him, 'Make things right for me. Someone is doing me wrong.'

"For some time the judge refused. But finally he said to himself, 'I don't have any respect for God. I don't care about people. But this widow keeps bothering me. So I will see that things are made right for her. If I don't, she will wear me out by coming again and again!'"

The Lord said, "Listen to what the unfair judge says.

"God's chosen people cry out to him day and night. Won't he make things right for them? Will he keep putting them off? I tell you, God will see that things are made right for them. He will make sure it happens quickly.

"But when the Son of Man comes, will he find people on earth who have faith?"

Jesus told a story to some people who were sure they were right with God. They looked down on everybody else. He said to them, "Two men went up to the temple to pray. One was a Pharisee. The other was a tax collector.

"The Pharisee stood up and prayed about himself. 'God, I thank you that I am not like other people,' he said. 'I am not like robbers or those who do other evil things. I am not like those who commit adultery. I am not even like this tax collector. I fast twice a week. And I give a tenth of all I get.'

"But the tax collector stood not very far away. He would not even look up to heaven. He beat his chest and said, 'God, have mercy on me. I am a sinner.'

"I tell you, the tax collector went home accepted by God. But not the Pharisee. Everyone who lifts himself up will be brought down. And anyone who is brought down will be lifted up."

When Jesus finished saying these things, he left Galilee. He went into the area of Judea on the other side of the Jordan River. Large crowds followed him. As usual, he taught them and he healed them there.

Some Pharisees came to put him to the test. They asked, "Does the Law allow a man to divorce his wife for any reason at all?"

Jesus replied, "Haven't you read that in the beginning the Creator 'made them male and female'? He said, 'That's why a man will leave his father and mother and be joined to his wife. The two will become one.'³ They are no longer two, but one. So a man must not separate what God has joined together."

They asked, "Then why did Moses command that a man can give his wife a letter of divorce and send her away?"

Jesus replied, "Moses let you divorce your wives because you were stubborn. But it was not this way from the beginning.

"The teachings of the Law and the Prophets were preached until John came. Since then, the good news of God's kingdom is being preached. And everyone is trying very hard to enter it. It is easier for heaven and earth to disappear than for the smallest part of a letter to drop out of the Law.

"Anyone who divorces his wife and gets married to another woman commits adultery. Also, the man who gets married to a divorced woman commits adultery. A man may divorce his wife only if she has not been faithful to him."

When they were in the house again, the disciples asked Jesus about this.

He answered, "What if a man divorces his wife and gets married to another woman? He commits adultery against her. And what if she divorces her husband and gets married to another man? She commits adultery."

The disciples said to him, "If that's the way it is between a husband and wife, it is better not to get married."

Jesus replied, "Not everyone can accept the idea of staying single. Only those who have been helped to live without getting married can accept it. Some men are not able to have children because they were born that way. Some have been made that way by other people. Others have made themselves that way in order to serve the kingdom of heaven. The one who can accept living that way should do it."

Some people brought little children to Jesus. They wanted him to place his hands on the children and pray for them. People were also bringing babies to Jesus. They wanted him to touch them. But the disciples told the people to stop.

When Jesus saw this, he was angry. He said to his disciples, "Let the little children come to me. Don't keep them away. God's kingdom belongs to people like them. What I'm about to tell you is true. Anyone who will not receive God's kingdom like a little child will never enter it."

Then he took the children in his arms. He put his hands on them and blessed them. Then he went on from there.

As Jesus started on his way, a man ran up to him. He fell on his knees before Jesus. "Good teacher," he said, "what must I do to receive eternal life?"

"Why do you call me good?" Jesus answered. "There is only One who is good. No one is good except God. If you want to enter the kingdom, obey the commandments."

"Which ones?" the man asked.

Jesus said, "'Do not commit murder. Do not commit adultery. Do not steal. Do not give false witness. Do not cheat. Honor your father and mother.' And 'love your neighbor as you love yourself.'"[4]

"Teacher," he said, "I have obeyed all those commandments since I was a boy. What else do I need to do?"

Jesus looked at him and loved him. "You are missing one thing," he said. "If you want to be perfect, go and sell everything you have.

Give the money to those who are poor. You will have treasure in heaven. Then come and follow me."

The man's face fell. He went away sad, because he was very rich.

Jesus looked around. He said to his disciples, "How hard it is for rich people to enter God's kingdom!"

The disciples were amazed at his words. But Jesus said again, "Children, how hard it is to enter God's kingdom! Is it hard for a camel to go through the eye of a needle? It is even harder for the rich to enter God's kingdom!"

The disciples were even more amazed. They said to each other, "Then who can be saved?"

Jesus looked at them and said, "With man, that is impossible. But not with God. All things are possible with God."

Peter answered him, "We have left everything to follow you! What reward will be given to us?"

"What I'm about to tell you is true," Jesus said to them. "When all things are made new, the Son of Man will sit on his glorious throne. Then you who have followed me will also sit on 12 thrones. You will judge the 12 tribes of Israel.

"Has anyone left home or family or fields for me and the good news? They will receive 100 times as much in this world. They will have homes and families and fields. But they will also be treated badly by others. In the world to come they will live forever. But many who are first will be last. And the last will be first.

"The kingdom of heaven is like a man who owned land. He went out early in the morning to hire people to work in his vineyard. He agreed to give them the usual pay for a day's work. Then he sent them into his vineyard.

"About nine o'clock in the morning he went out again. He saw others standing in the marketplace doing nothing. He told them, 'You also go and work in my vineyard. I'll pay you what is right.' So they went.

"He went out again about noon and at three o'clock and did the same thing. About five o'clock he went out and found still others standing around. He asked them, 'Why have you been standing here all day long doing nothing?'

"'Because no one has hired us,' they answered.

"He said to them, 'You also go and work in my vineyard.'

"When evening came, the owner of the vineyard spoke to the person who was in charge of the workers. He said, 'Call the workers and give them their pay. Begin with the last ones I hired. Then go on to the first ones.'

"The workers who were hired about five o'clock came. Each received the usual day's pay. So when those who were hired first came, they expected to receive more. But each of them also received the usual day's pay.

"When they received it, they began to complain about the owner. 'These people who were hired last worked only one hour,' they said. 'You have paid them the same as us. We have done most of the work and have been in the hot sun all day.'

"The owner answered one of them. 'Friend,' he said, 'I'm being fair to you. Didn't you agree to work for the usual day's pay? Take your money and go. I want to give the ones I hired last the same pay I gave you. Don't I have the right to do what I want with my own money? Do you feel cheated because I gave so freely to the others?'

"So those who are last will be first. And those who are first will be last."

They were on their way up to Jerusalem. Jesus was leading the way. On the way, he took the 12 disciples to one side to talk to them. He told them what was going to happen to him.

"We are going up to Jerusalem," he said. "Everything that the prophets wrote about the Son of Man will come true. The Son of Man will be handed over to the chief priests and the teachers of the law. They will sentence him to death. Then they will hand him over to people who are not Jews. They will make fun of him. They will laugh at him and spit on him. They will whip him and kill him. They will nail him to a cross. On the third day, he will rise from the dead!"

The disciples did not understand any of this. Its meaning was hidden from them. So they didn't know what Jesus was talking about.

The mother of Zebedee's sons came to Jesus. Her sons came with her. Getting on her knees, she asked a favor of him.

"What do you want me to do for you?" he asked.

She said, "Promise me that one of my two sons may sit at your right hand in your kingdom. Promise that the other one may sit at your left hand."

"You don't know what you're asking for," Jesus said. "Can you drink the cup of suffering I drink? Or can you go through the baptism of suffering I must go through?"

"We can," they answered.

Jesus said to them, "You will drink the cup I drink. And you will go through the baptism I go through. But it is not for me to say who will sit at my right or left hand. These places belong to those my Father has prepared them for."

The other ten disciples heard about this. They became angry at James and John.

Jesus called them together. He said, "You know about those who are rulers of the nations. They hold power over their people. Their high officials order them around. Don't be like that. Instead, anyone who wants to be important among you must be your servant. And anyone who wants to be first must be the slave of everyone.

"Be like the Son of Man. He did not come to be served. Instead, he came to serve others. He came to give his life as the price for setting many people free."

Jesus and his disciples came to Jericho. They were leaving the city. A large crowd was with them.

A blind man was sitting by the side of the road begging. His name was Bartimaeus. Bartimaeus means Son of Timaeus. The blind man heard the crowd going by. He asked what was happening. They told him, "Jesus of Nazareth is passing by."

So the blind man called out, "Jesus! Son of David! Have mercy on me!"

Many people commanded him to stop. They told him to be quiet. But he shouted even louder, "Son of David! Have mercy on me!"

Jesus stopped and said, "Call for him."

So they called out to the blind man, "Cheer up! Get up on your feet! Jesus is calling for you."

He threw his coat to one side. Then he jumped to his feet and came to Jesus.

"What do you want me to do for you?" Jesus asked him.

"Lord, I want to be able to see," the blind man replied.

Jesus said to him, "Receive your sight. Your faith has healed you."

Right away he could see. He followed Jesus, praising God. When all the people saw it, they also praised God.

Jesus entered Jericho and was passing through. A man named Zacchaeus lived there. He was a chief tax collector and was very rich.

Zacchaeus wanted to see who Jesus was. But he was a short man. He could not see Jesus because of the crowd. So he ran ahead and climbed a sycamore-fig tree. He wanted to see Jesus, who was coming that way.

Jesus reached the spot where Zacchaeus was. He looked up and said, "Zacchaeus, come down at once. I must stay at your house today." So Zacchaeus came down at once and welcomed him gladly.

All the people saw this. They began to whisper among themselves. They said, "Jesus has gone to be the guest of a 'sinner.'"

But Zacchaeus stood up. He said, "Look, Lord! Here and now I give half of what I own to those who are poor. And if I have cheated anybody out of anything, I will pay it back. I will pay back four times the amount I took."

Jesus said to Zacchaeus, "Today salvation has come to your house. You are a member of Abraham's family line. The Son of Man came to look for the lost and save them."

While the people were listening to these things, Jesus told them a story. He was near Jerusalem. The people thought that God's kingdom was going to appear right away.

Jesus said, "A man from an important family went to a country far away. He went there to be made king and then return home. So he sent for ten of his servants. He gave them each about three months' pay. 'Put this money to work until I come back,' he said.

"But those he ruled over hated him. They sent some messengers after him. They were sent to say, 'We don't want this man to be our king.'

"But he was made king and returned home. Then he sent for the servants he had given the money to. He wanted to find out what they had earned with it.

"The first one came to him. He said, 'Sir, your money has earned ten times as much.'

"'You have done well, my good servant!' his master replied. 'You have been faithful in a very small matter. So I will put you in charge of ten towns.'

"The second servant came to his master. He said, 'Sir, your money has earned five times as much.'

"His master answered, 'I will put you in charge of five towns.'

"Then another servant came. He said, 'Sir, here is your money. I have kept it hidden in a piece of cloth. I was afraid of you. You are a hard man. You take out what you did not put in. You harvest what you did not plant.'

"His master replied, 'I will judge you by your own words, you evil servant! So you knew that I am a hard man? You knew that I take out what I did not put in? You knew that I harvest what I did not plant? Then why didn't you put my money in the bank? When I came back, I could have collected it with interest.'

"Then he said to those standing by, 'Take his money away from him. Give it to the one who has ten times as much.'

"'Sir,' they said, 'he already has ten times as much!'

"He replied, 'I tell you that everyone who has will be given more. But here is what will happen to anyone who has nothing. Even what he has will be taken away from him. And what about my enemies who did not want me to be king over them? Bring them here! Kill them in front of me!'"

It was six days before the Passover Feast. Jesus arrived at Bethany, where Lazarus lived. Lazarus was the one Jesus had raised from the dead. A dinner was given at Bethany to honor Jesus. He was at the table in the home of a man named Simon, who had a skin desease. Martha served the food. Lazarus was among those at the table with Jesus.

Then Mary took about a pint of pure nard.[5] It was an expensive perfume. She broke the jar open and poured the perfume on Jesus' head. She poured it on Jesus' feet and wiped them with her hair. The house was filled with the sweet smell of the perfume.

But Judas Iscariot didn't like what Mary did. He was one of Jesus' disciples. Later he was going to hand Jesus over to his enemies. Judas said, "Why wasn't this perfume sold? Why wasn't the money given to poor people? It was worth a year's pay."

He didn't say this because he cared about the poor. He said it because he was a thief. Judas was in charge of the money bag. He used to help himself to what was in it.

Some of the people there became angry. They said to one another, "Why waste this perfume? The perfume could have been sold at a high price. The money could have been given to poor people." So they found fault with the woman.

Jesus was aware of this. "Leave her alone," Jesus replied. "Why are you bothering her? She has done a beautiful thing to me. You will always have poor people with you. You can help them any-time you want to. But you will not always have me. She did what she could. She poured perfume on my body to prepare me to be buried. What I'm about to tell you is true. What she has done will be told anywhere the good news is preached all over the world. It will be told in memory of her."

Meanwhile a large crowd of Jews found out that Jesus was there, so they came. But they did not come only because of Jesus. They also came to see Lazarus. After all, Jesus had raised him from the dead.

So the chief priests made plans to kill Lazarus too. Because of Lazarus, many of the Jews were starting to follow Jesus. They were putting their faith in him.

As they all approached Jerusalem, they came to Bethphage. It was on the Mount of Olives. Jesus sent out two of his disciples. He said to them, "Go to the village ahead of you. As soon as you get there, you will find a donkey tied up. Her colt will be with her. No one has ever ridden it. Untie it and bring it here. Someone may ask you, 'Why are you doing this?' If so, say, 'The Lord needs it. But he will send it back here soon.'"

This took place so that what was spoken through the prophet would come true. It says,

"Say to the city of Zion,

'See, your king comes to you.

He is gentle and riding on a donkey.

He is riding on a donkey's colt.'"[6]

The disciples went and did what Jesus told them to do. They found a colt out in the street. It was there just as Jesus had told them. It was tied at a doorway. They untied it. Some people stand-ing there asked, "What are you doing? Why are you untying that colt?"

They answered as Jesus had told them to. So the people let them go.

They brought the colt to Jesus. They threw their coats over it. Then Jesus sat on the coats.

The large crowd that had come for the Feast heard that Jesus was on his way to Jerusalem. So they took branches from palm trees and went out to meet him. As he went along, people spread their coats on the road. Others spread branches they had cut in the fields. Some of the people went ahead of him, and some followed. They all shouted,

"Hosanna to the Son of David![7]

"Blessed is the one who comes in the name of the Lord!

"Blessed is the coming kingdom of our father David!

"Blessed is the King of Israel!

"May there be peace and glory in the highest heaven!

"Hosanna in the highest heaven!"

Jesus came near the place where the road goes down the Mount of Olives. There the whole crowd of disciples began to praise God with joy. In loud voices they praised him for all the miracles they had seen.

Some of the Pharisees in the crowd spoke to Jesus. "Teacher," they said, "tell your disciples to stop!"

"I tell you," he replied, "if they keep quiet, the stones will cry out."

At first, Jesus' disciples did not understand all this. They realized it only after he had received glory. Then they realized that these things had been written about him. They realized that the people had done these things to him.

A crowd had been with Jesus when he called Lazarus from the tomb and raised him from the dead. So they continued to tell everyone about what had happened. Many people went out to meet him. They had heard that he had done this miraculous sign.

So the Pharisees said to one another, "This isn't getting us anywhere. Look how the whole world is following him!"

chapter fifteen

Authority Questioned

J esus approached Jerusalem. When he saw the city, he began to sob. He said, "I wish you had known today what would bring you peace! But now it is hidden from your eyes.

"The days will come when your enemies will arrive. They will build a wall of dirt up against your city. They will surround you and close you in on every side. You didn't recognize the time when God came to you. So your enemies will smash you to the ground. They will destroy you and all the people inside your walls. They will not leave one stone on top of another."

When Jesus entered Jerusalem, the whole city was stirred up. The people asked, "Who is this?"

The crowds answered, "This is Jesus. He is the prophet from Nazareth in Galilee."

He looked around at everything. But it was already late. So he went out to Bethany with the Twelve.

The next day as Jesus and his disciples were leaving Bethany, they were hungry. Not too far away, he saw a fig tree. It was covered in leaves. He went to find out if it had any fruit. When he reached it, he found nothing but leaves. It was not the season for figs.

Then Jesus said to the tree, "May no one ever eat fruit from you again!" And his disciples heard him say it. Right away the tree dried up.

When Jesus reached Jerusalem, he entered the temple area. He began chasing out those who were buying and selling there. He turned over the tables of the people who were exchanging money. He also turned over the benches of those who were selling doves. He would not allow anyone to carry items for sale through the temple courtyards.

Then he taught them. He told them, "It is written that the Lord said,

"'My house will be called

a house where people from all nations can pray.'

But you have made it a 'den for robbers.'"[1]

The chief priests and the teachers of the law heard about this. They began looking for a way to kill Jesus. They were afraid of him, because the whole crowd was amazed at his teaching.

Every day Jesus was teaching at the temple. But the chief priests and the teachers of the law were trying to kill him. So were the leaders among the people. But they couldn't find any way to do it. All the people were paying close attention to his words.

Blind people and those who were disabled came to Jesus at the temple. There he healed them. The chief priests and the teachers of the law saw the wonderful things he did. They also saw the children in the temple area shouting, "Hosanna to the Son of David!" But when they saw all of this, they became angry.

"Do you hear what these children are saying?" they asked him.

"Yes," replied Jesus. "Haven't you ever read about it in Scripture? It says,

"'You have made sure that children and infants

praise you.'"[2]

Jesus had done all these miraculous signs in front of them. But they still would not believe in him. This happened as Isaiah the prophet had said it would. He had said,

"Lord, who has believed what we've been saying?

Who has seen the Lord's saving power?"[3]

For this reason, they could not believe. As Isaiah says in another place,

"The Lord has blinded their eyes.

He has closed their minds.

So they can't see with their eyes.

They can't understand with their minds.

They can't turn to the Lord. If they could, he

would heal them."[4]

Isaiah said this because he saw Jesus' glory and spoke about him.

At the same time that Jesus did those miracles, many of the leaders believed in him. But because of the Pharisees, they would not admit they believed. They were afraid they would be thrown out of the synagogue. They loved praise from people more than praise from God.

Then Jesus cried out, "Anyone who believes in me does not believe in me only. He also believes in the One who sent me. When he looks at me, he sees the One who sent me.

"I have come into the world to be a light. No one who believes in me will stay in darkness.

"I don't judge a person who hears my words but does not obey them. I didn't come to judge the world. I came to save it. But there is a judge for anyone who does not accept me and my words. The very words I have spoken will judge him on the last day.

"I did not speak on my own. The Father who sent me commanded me what to say. He also told me how to say it. I know that his command leads to eternal life. So everything I say is just what the Father has told me to say."

There were some Greeks among the people who went up to worship during the Feast. They came to ask Philip for a favor. Philip was from Bethsaida in Galilee.

"Sir," they said, "we would like to see Jesus."

Philip went to tell Andrew. Then Andrew and Philip told Jesus.

Jesus replied, "The hour has come for the Son of Man to receive glory. What I'm about to tell you is true. Unless a grain of wheat falls to the ground and dies, it remains only one seed. But if it dies, it produces many seeds.

"Anyone who loves his life will lose it. But anyone who hates his life in this world will keep it and have eternal life. Anyone who serves me must follow me. And where I am, my servant will also be. My Father will honor the one who serves me.

"My heart is troubled. What should I say? 'Father, save me from this hour'? No. This is the very reason I came. Father, bring glory to your name!"

Then a voice came from heaven. It said, "I have brought glory to my name. I will bring glory to it again."

The crowd there heard the voice. Some said it was thunder. Others said an angel had spoken to Jesus.

Jesus said, "This voice was for your benefit, not mine. Now it is time for the world to be judged. Now the prince of this world will be thrown out. But I am going to be lifted up from the earth. When I am, I will bring all people to myself." He said this to show them how he was going to die.

The crowd spoke up. "The Law tells us that the Christ will remain forever," they said. "So how can you say, 'The Son of Man must be lifted up'? Who is this 'Son of Man'?"

Then Jesus told them, "You are going to have the light just a little while longer. Walk while you have the light. Do this before darkness catches up with you. Anyone who walks in the dark does not know where he is going. While you have the light, put your trust in it. Then you can become sons of light."

When Jesus had finished speaking, he left and hid from them.

When evening came, Jesus and his disciples left the city. In the morning, as Jesus and his disciples walked along, they saw the fig tree. It was dried up all the way down to the roots.

When the disciples saw this, they were amazed. "How did the fig tree dry up so quickly?" they asked.

Peter remembered. He said to Jesus, "Rabbi, look! The fig tree you put a curse on has dried up!"

Jesus replied, "What I'm about to tell you is true. You must have faith and not doubt. Then you can do what was done to the fig tree.

And you can say to this mountain, 'Go and throw yourself into the sea.' It will be done. If you believe, you will receive what you ask for when you pray.

"So I tell you, when you pray for something, believe that you have already received it. Then it will be yours. And when you stand praying, forgive anyone you have anything against. Then your Father in heaven will forgive your sins."

Jesus and his disciples arrived again in Jerusalem. Jesus was teaching the people in the temple courtyard. He was preaching the good news to them.

The chief priests and the teachers of the law came up to him. The elders came with them. "Tell us by what authority you are doing these things," they all said. "Who gave you this authority?"

Jesus replied, "I will also ask you one question. If you answer me, I will tell you by what authority I am doing these things. Where did John's baptism come from? Was it from heaven? Or did it come from men?"

They talked to each other about it. They said, "If we say, 'From heaven,' he will ask, 'Then why didn't you believe him?' But if we say, 'From men' all the people will throw stones at us and kill us. We are afraid of the people. Everyone believes that John was a prophet."

So they answered Jesus, "We don't know."

Jesus said, "Then I won't tell you by what authority I am doing these things either."

Jesus went on to tell the people a story. "What do you think about this? A man had two sons. He went to the first and said, 'Son, go and work today in the vineyard.'

"'I will not,' the son answered. But later he changed his mind and went.

"Then the father went to the other son. He said the same thing. The son answered, 'I will, sir.' But he did not go.

"Which of the two sons did what his father wanted?"

"The first," they answered.

Jesus said to them, "What I'm about to tell you is true. Tax collectors and prostitutes will enter the kingdom of God ahead of you. John came to show you the right way to live. And you did not believe him. But the tax collectors and the prostitutes did. You saw this. But even then you did not turn away from your sins and believe him.

"Listen to another story. A man who owned some land planted a vineyard. He put a wall around it. He dug a pit for a winepress in it. He also built a lookout tower. He rented the vineyard out to some farmers. Then he went away on a journey.

"At harvest time he sent a servant to the renters. They were supposed to give him some of the fruit of the vineyard. But they grabbed the servant and beat him up. Then they sent him away with nothing. So the man sent another servant to the renters. They hit this one on the head and treated him badly. The man sent still another servant. The renters killed him. The man sent many others. The renters beat up some of them. They killed the others.

"Then the owner of the vineyard said, 'What should I do? I have a son, and I love him. I will send him. Maybe they will respect him.'

"But the renters saw the son coming. They said to each other, 'This is the one who will receive all the owner's property someday. Come, let's kill him. Then everything will be ours.' So they took him and threw him out of the vineyard. Then they killed him.

"When the owner of the vineyard comes back, what will he do to those renters?"

"He will destroy those evil people," they replied. "Then he will rent the vineyard out to other renters. They will give him his share of the crop at harvest time."

When the people heard this, they said, "We hope this never happens!"

Jesus said to them, "Haven't you ever read what the Scriptures say,

"'The stone the builders didn't accept

has become the most important stone of all.

The Lord has done it.

It is wonderful in our eyes'?[5]

"So here is what I tell you. The kingdom of God will be taken away from you. It will be given to people who will produce its fruit. Everyone who falls on that stone will be broken to pieces. But the stone will crush anyone it falls on."

The chief priests and the Pharisees heard Jesus' stories. They knew he was talking about them. So they looked for a way to arrest him. But they were afraid of the crowd. The people believed that Jesus was a prophet.

Jesus told them more stories. He said, "Here is what the kingdom of heaven is like. A king prepared a wedding dinner for his son. He sent his servants to those who had been invited to the dinner. The servants told them to come. But they refused.

"Then he sent some more servants. He said, 'Tell those who were invited that I have prepared my dinner. I have killed my oxen and my fattest cattle. Everything is ready. Come to the wedding dinner.'

"But the people paid no attention. One went away to his field. Another went away to his business. The rest grabbed his servants. They treated them badly and then killed them.

"The king became very angry. He sent his army to destroy them. They killed those murderers and burned their city.

"Then the king said to his servants, 'The wedding dinner is ready. But those I invited were not fit to come. Go to the street corners. Invite to the dinner anyone you can find.' So the servants went out into the streets. They gathered all the people they could find, both good and bad. Soon the wedding hall was filled with guests.

"The king came in to see the guests. He noticed a man there who was not wearing wedding clothes. 'Friend,' he asked, 'how did you get in here without wedding clothes?' The man couldn't think of anything to say.

"Then the king told his servants, 'Tie up his hands and feet. Throw him outside into the darkness. Out there people will sob and grind their teeth.'

"Many are invited, but few are chosen."

The Pharisees went out. They made plans to trap Jesus with his own words. The religious leaders sent spies to keep a close watch on Jesus. They sent their followers to him. They sent the Herodians with them. The spies pretended to be honest. They hoped they could trap Jesus with something he would say. Then they could hand him over to the power and authority of the governor.

So the spies questioned Jesus. "Teacher," they said, "we know you are a man of honor. You teach the way of God truthfully. You don't let others tell you what to do or say. You don't care how important they are. Tell us then, what do you think? Is it right to pay taxes to Caesar or not?"

But Jesus knew their evil plans. He said, "You pretenders! Why are you trying to trap me? Show me the coin people use for paying the tax."

They brought him a silver coin.

He asked them, "Whose picture is this? And whose words?"

"Caesar's," they replied.

Then he said to them, "Give to Caesar what belongs to Caesar. And give to God what belongs to God."

When they heard this, they were amazed. They were not able to trap him with what he had said there in front of all the people. So they left him and went away.

That same day the Sadducees came to Jesus with a question. They do not believe that people rise from the dead.

"Teacher," they said, "Moses wrote for us about a man's brother who dies. Suppose the brother leaves a wife but has no children. Then the man must get married to the widow. He must have children to carry on his dead brother's name.[6]

"There were seven brothers. The first one got married to a woman. He died without leaving any children. The second one got married to the widow. He also died and left no child. It was the same with the third one. It happened right on down to the seventh brother. In fact, none of the seven left any children. Last of all, the woman died too. Now then, when the dead rise, whose wife will she be? All seven brothers were married to her."

Jesus replied, "You are mistaken, because you do not know the Scriptures. And you do not know the power of God.

"People in this world get married. And their parents give them to get married. But it will not be like that when the dead rise. Those who are considered worthy to take part in what happens at that time won't get married. And their parents won't give them to be married. They can't die anymore. They are God's children. They will be given a new form of life when the dead rise. They will be like the angels in heaven.

"What about the dead rising? Even Moses showed that the dead rise. Haven't you read in the scroll of Moses the story of the bush? God said to Moses, 'I am the God of Abraham. I am the God of Isaac. And I am the God of Jacob.'[7]

"He is not the God of the dead. He is the God of the living. In his eyes, everyone is alive. You have made a big mistake!"

When the crowds heard this, they were amazed by what he taught. Some of the teachers of the law replied, "You have spoken well, teacher!"

The Pharisees heard that the Sadducees weren't able to answer Jesus. So the Pharisees got together. One of them was an authority on the law. He noticed that Jesus had given the Sadducees a good answer. So he tested Jesus with a question. "Teacher," he asked, "which is the most important commandment in the Law?"

Jesus answered, "Here is the most important one. Moses said, 'Israel, listen to me. The Lord is our God. The Lord is one. Love the Lord your God with all your heart and with all your soul. Love him with all your mind and with all your strength.'[8] This is the first and most important commandment.

"And here is the second one. 'Love your neighbor as you love yourself.'[9] There is no commandment more important than these. Everything that is written in the Law and the Prophets is based on these two commandments."

"You have spoken well, teacher," the man replied. "You are right in saying that God is one. There is no other God but him. To love God with all your heart and mind and strength is very important. So is loving your neighbor as you love yourself. These things are more important than all burnt offerings and sacrifices."

Jesus saw that the man had answered wisely. He said to him, "You are not far from God's kingdom."

From then on, no one dared to ask Jesus any more questions.

Jesus was teaching in the temple courtyard. The Pharisees were gathered together. Jesus asked them, "What do you think about the Christ? Whose son is he?"

"The son of David," they replied.

He said to them, "Then why does David call him 'Lord'? The Holy Spirit spoke through David himself. David said,

"'The Lord said to my Lord,

"Sit at my right hand

until I put your enemies

under your control."'[10]

So if David calls him 'Lord,' how can he be David's son?"

No one could answer him with a single word. The large crowd listened to Jesus with delight.

Jesus spoke to the crowds and to his disciples. All the people were listening.

"The teachers of the law and the Pharisees sit in Moses' seat," he said. "So you must obey them. Do everything they tell you. But don't do what they do. They don't practice what they preach. They tie up heavy loads and put them on other people's shoulders. But they themselves aren't willing to lift a finger to move them. They take over the houses of widows.

"Watch out for the teachers of the law. Everything they do is done for others to see.

"They like to walk around in long robes. On their foreheads and arms they wear little boxes that hold Scripture verses. They make the boxes very wide. And they make the tassels on their coats very long. They say long prayers to show off. God will punish those men very much.

"They love to sit down in the place of honor at dinners. They also love to have the most important seats in the synagogues. They love to be greeted in the marketplaces. They love it when people call them 'Rabbi.'

"But you shouldn't be called 'Rabbi.' You have only one Master, and you are all brothers. Do not call anyone on earth 'father.' You have one Father, and he is in heaven. You shouldn't be called 'teacher.' You have one Teacher, and he is the Christ. The most important person among you will be your servant. Anyone who lifts himself up will be brought down. And anyone who is brought down will be lifted up.

chapter sixteen

Talking About the Future

Jesus sat down across from the place where people put their temple offerings. He watched the crowd putting their money into the offering boxes. Many rich people threw large amounts into them.

But a poor widow came and put in two very small copper coins. They were worth much less than a penny.

Jesus asked his disciples to come to him. He said, "What I'm about to tell you is true. That poor widow has put more into the offering box than all the others. They all gave a lot because they are rich. But even though she is poor, she put in everything she had. She gave all she had to live on."

Jesus left the temple. He was walking away when his disciples came up to him. They wanted to call his attention to the temple buildings. They spoke about how it was decorated with beautiful stones and with gifts that honored God.

One of his disciples said to him, "Look, Teacher! What huge stones! What wonderful buildings!"

But Jesus asked, "Do you see all this? The time will come when not one stone will be left on top of another. Every stone will be thrown down."

Jesus was sitting on the Mount of Olives, across from the temple. Peter, James, John and Andrew asked him a question in private.

"Tell us," they said. "When will this happen? And what will be the sign of your coming? What will be the sign of the end?"

Jesus answered, "Keep watch! Be careful that no one fools you. Many will come in my name. They will claim, 'I am the Christ!' And they will say, 'The time is near!' They will fool many people. Do not follow them.

"You will hear about wars. You will also hear people talking about future wars. Don't be alarmed. Those things must happen first. But the end will not come right away."

Then Jesus said to them, "Nation will fight against nation. Kingdom will fight against kingdom. In many places there will be powerful earthquakes. People will go hungry. There will be terrible sicknesses. Things will happen that will make people afraid. There will be great and miraculous signs from heaven. All these are the beginning of birth pains.

"This good news of the kingdom will be preached in the whole world. It will be a witness to all nations. Then the end will come.

"But before all this, people will arrest you and treat you badly. You will be handed over to the local courts. You will be whipped in the synagogues. You will stand in front of governors and kings because of me. In that way you will be witnesses to them. All nations will hate you because of me.

"At that time, many will turn away from their faith. They will hate each other. They will hand each other over to their enemies. Many false prophets will appear. They will fool many people. Because evil will grow, most people's love will grow cold. But the one who stands firm to the end will be saved.

"You will be arrested and brought to trial. But make up your mind not to worry ahead of time about how to stand up for your-selves. Just say what God brings to your mind at the time. It is not you speaking, but the Holy Spirit. I will give you words of wisdom. None of your enemies will be able to withstand them or oppose them.

"Even your parents, brothers, sisters, relatives and friends will hand you over to the authorities. Brothers will hand over brothers to be killed. Fathers will hand over their children. Children will rise up against their parents and have them put to death. Everyone will hate you because of me. But not a hair on your head will be harmed. If you stand firm, you will gain life.

"A time is coming when you will see armies surround Jerusalem. Then you will know that it will soon be destroyed.

"The prophet Daniel spoke about 'the hated thing that destroys.'[1] Someday you will see it standing in the holy place. The reader should understand this.

"Then those who are in Judea should escape to the mountains. Those in the city should get out. Those in the country should not enter the city. No one on the roof should go down into his house to take anything out. No one in the field should go back to get his coat. This is the time when God will punish Jerusalem. Everything will come true, just as it has been written.

"How awful it will be in those days for pregnant women! How awful for nursing mothers! There will be terrible suffering in the land. There will be great anger against those people. Some will be killed by the sword. Others will be taken as prisoners to all the nations. Jerusalem will be overrun by those who aren't Jews until the times of the non-Jews come to an end.[2]

"Pray that you will not have to escape in winter or on the Sabbath day. There will be terrible suffering in those days. It will be worse than any other from the beginning of the world until now. And there will never be anything like it again. If the time had not been cut short, no one would live. But because of God's chosen people, it will be shortened.

"At that time someone may say to you, 'Look! Here is the Christ!' Or, 'Look! There he is!' Do not believe it. False Christs and false prophets will appear. They will do signs and miracles. They will try to fool God's chosen people if possible. Keep watch! I have told you everything ahead of time.

"So if anyone tells you, 'He is far out in the desert,' do not go out there. Or if anyone says, 'He is deep inside the house,' do not believe it. Lightning that comes from the east can be seen in the west. It will be the same when the Son of Man comes. The vultures will gather wherever there is a dead body.

"So in those days there will be terrible suffering. After that, Scripture says,

"'The sun will be darkened.

The moon will not shine.

The stars will fall from the sky.

The heavenly bodies will be shaken.'[3]

"The nations of the earth will be in terrible pain. They will be puzzled by the roaring and tossing of the sea. Terror will make people faint. They will be worried about what is happening in the world. The sun, moon and stars will be shaken from their places.

"At that time the sign of the Son of Man will appear in the sky. All the nations on earth will be sad. They will see the Son of Man coming on the clouds of the sky. He will come with power and great glory. He will send his angels with a loud trumpet call. They will gather his chosen people from all four directions. They will bring them from one end of the heavens to the other.

"When these things begin to take place, stand up. Hold your head up with joy and hope. The time when you will be set free will be very close."

Jesus told them a story. "Learn a lesson from the fig tree. As soon as its twigs get tender and its leaves come out, you know that summer is near. In the same way, when you see all those things happening, you will know that the end is near. It is right at the door.

"What I'm about to tell you is true. The people living at that time will certainly not pass away until all these things have happened. Heaven and earth will pass away. But my words will never pass away.

"Be careful. If you aren't, your hearts will be loaded down with wasteful living, drunkenness and the worries of life. Then the day the Son of Man returns will close on you like a trap. You will not be expecting it. That day will come upon every person who lives on the whole earth.

"Always keep watching. Pray that you will be able to escape all that is about to happen. Also, pray that you will not be judged guilty when the Son of Man comes.

"No one knows about that day or hour. Not even the angels in heaven know. The Son does not know. Only the Father knows.

"Remember how it was in the days of Noah. It will be the same when the Son of Man comes.

"In the days before the flood, people were eating and drinking. They were getting married. They were giving their daughters to be married. They did all those things right up to the day Noah entered the ark. They knew nothing about what would happen until the flood came and took them all away. That is how it will be when the Son of Man comes.

"Two men will be in the field. One will be taken and the other left. Two women will be grinding with a hand mill. One will be taken and the other left.

"So keep watch. You do not know on what day your Lord will come.

"Be dressed and ready to serve. Keep your lamps burning. Be like servants waiting for their master to return from a wedding dinner. When he comes and knocks, they can open the door for him at once.

"It will be good for those servants whose master finds them ready when he comes. What I'm about to tell you is true. The master will then dress himself so he can serve them. He will have them take their places at the table. And he will come and wait on them. It will be good for those servants whose master finds them ready. It will even be good if he comes very late at night.

"But here is what you must understand. Suppose the owner of the house knew at what time of night the robber was coming. Then he would have kept watch. He would not have let his house be broken into. So you also must be ready. The Son of Man will come at an hour when you don't expect him."

Peter asked, "Lord, are you telling this story to us, or to everyone?"

The Lord answered, "Suppose a master puts one of his servants in charge of his other servants. The servant's job is to give them the food they are to receive at the right time. The master wants a faithful and wise manager for this. It will be good for the servant if the master finds him doing his job when the master returns. What I'm about to tell you is true. The master will put that servant in charge of everything he owns.

"But suppose the servant says to himself, 'My master is taking a long time to come back.' Suppose he begins to beat the other servants. Suppose he feeds himself. And suppose he drinks until he gets drunk. The master of that servant will come back on a day the servant doesn't expect him. He will return at an hour the servant doesn't know. Then the master will cut him to pieces. He will send him to the place where unbelievers go. There people will sob and grind their teeth.

"Suppose a servant knows his master's wishes. But he doesn't get ready. And he doesn't do what his master wants. That servant will be beaten with many blows.

"But suppose the servant does not know his master's wishes. And suppose he does things for which he should be punished. He will be beaten with only a few blows.

"Much will be required of everyone who has been given much. Even more will be asked of the person who is supposed to take care of much.

"So keep watch! You do not know when the owner of the house will come back. It may be in the evening or at midnight. It may be when the rooster crows or at dawn. He may come suddenly. So do not let him find you sleeping.

"What I say to you, I say to everyone. 'Watch!'

"Here is what the kingdom of heaven will be like at that time. Ten bridesmaids took their lamps and went out to meet the groom. Five of them were foolish. Five were wise. The foolish ones took their lamps but didn't take any olive oil with them. The wise ones took oil in jars along with their lamps. The groom did not come for a long time. So the bridesmaids all grew tired and fell asleep.

"At midnight someone cried out, 'Here's the groom! Come out to meet him!'

"Then all the bridesmaids woke up and got their lamps ready. The foolish ones said to the wise ones, 'Give us some of your oil. Our lamps are going out.'

"'No,' they replied. 'There may not be enough for all of us. Instead, go to those who sell oil. Buy some for yourselves.'

"So they went to buy the oil. But while they were on their way, the groom arrived. The bridesmaids who were ready went in with him to the wedding dinner. Then the door was shut.

"Later, the other bridesmaids also came. 'Sir! Sir!' they said. 'Open the door for us!'

"But he replied, 'What I'm about to tell you is true. I don't know you.'

"So keep watch. You do not know the day or the hour that the groom will come.

"Again, here is what the kingdom of heaven will be like. A man was going on a journey. He sent for his servants and put them in charge of his property. He gave $10,000 to one. He gave $4,000 to another. And he gave $2,000 to the third. The man gave each servant the amount of money he knew the servant could take care of. Then he went on his journey.

"The servant who had received the $10,000 went at once and put his money to work. He earned $10,000 more. The one with the $4,000 earned $4,000 more. But the man who had received $2,000 went and dug a hole in the ground. He hid his master's money in it.

"After a long time the master of those servants returned. He wanted to collect all the money they had earned. The man who had received $10,000 brought the other $10,000. 'Master,' he said, 'you trusted me with $10,000. See, I have earned $10,000 more.'

"His master replied, 'You have done well, good and faithful servant! You have been faithful with a few things. I will put you in charge of many things. Come and share your master's happiness!'

"The man with $4,000 also came. 'Master,' he said, 'you trusted me with $4,000. See, I have earned $4,000 more.'

"His master replied, 'You have done well, good and faithful servant! You have been faithful with a few things. I will put you in charge of many things. Come and share your master's happiness!'

"Then the man who had received $2,000 came. 'Master,' he said, 'I knew that you are a hard man. You harvest where you have not planted. You gather crops where you have not scattered seed. So I was afraid. I went out and hid your $2,000 in the ground. See, here is what belongs to you.'

"His master replied, 'You evil, lazy servant! So you knew that I harvest where I have not planted? You knew that I gather crops where I have not scattered seed? Well then, you should have put my money in the bank. When I returned, I would have received it back with interest.'

"Then his master commanded the other servants, 'Take the $2,000 from him. Give it to the one who has $20,000. Everyone who has will be given more. He will have more than enough. And what about anyone who doesn't have? Even what he has will be taken away from him. Throw that worthless servant outside. There in the darkness, people will sob and grind their teeth.'

"The Son of Man will come in all his glory. All the angels will come with him. Then he will sit on his throne in the glory of heaven. All the nations will be gathered in front of him. He will separate the people into two groups. He will be like a shepherd who separates the sheep from the goats. He will put the sheep to his right and the goats to his left.

"Then the King will speak to those on his right. He will say, 'My Father has blessed you. Come and take what is yours. It is the kingdom prepared for you since the world was created. I was hungry. And you gave me something to eat. I was thirsty. And you gave me something to drink. I was a stranger. And you invited me in. I needed clothes. And you gave them to me. I was sick. And you took care of me. I was in prison. And you came to visit me.'

"Then the people who have done what is right will answer him. 'Lord,' they will ask, 'when did we see you hungry and feed you? When did we see you thirsty and give you something to drink? When did we see you as a stranger and invite you in? When did we see you needing clothes and give them to you? When did we see you sick or in prison and go to visit you?'

"The King will reply, 'What I'm about to tell you is true. Anything you did for one of the least important of these brothers of mine, you did for me.'

"Then he will say to those on his left, 'You are cursed! Go away from me into the fire that burns forever. It has been prepared for the devil and his angels. I was hungry. But you gave me nothing to eat. I was thirsty. But you gave me nothing to drink. I was a stranger. But you did not invite me in. I needed clothes. But you did not give me any. I was sick and in prison. But you did not take care of me.'

"They also will answer, 'Lord, when did we see you hungry or thirsty and not help you? When did we see you as a stranger or needing clothes or sick or in prison and not help you?'

"He will reply, 'What I'm about to tell you is true. Anything you didn't do for one of the least important of these, you didn't do for me.'

"Then they will go away to be punished forever. But those who have done what is right will receive eternal life."

Jesus finished saying all these things. Then he said to his disciples, "As you know, the Passover Feast is two days away. The Son of Man will be handed over to be nailed to a cross."

chapter seventeen

Betrayed by a Friend

Each day Jesus taught at the temple. And each evening he went to spend the night on the hill called the Mount of Olives. All the people came to the temple early in the morning. They wanted to hear Jesus speak.

The Passover and the Feast of Unleavened Bread were only two days away. The chief priests and the teachers of the law were looking for a way to get rid of Jesus. They were afraid of the people.

Then the chief priests met with the elders of the people. They met in the palace of Caiaphas, the high priest. They made plans to arrest Jesus in a clever way. They wanted to kill him. "But not during the Feast," they said. "The people may stir up trouble."

Then Satan entered Judas, who was called Iscariot. Judas was one of the Twelve. He went to the chief priests and the officers of the temple guard. He talked with them about how he could hand Jesus over to them. They were delighted and agreed to give him money.

He asked, "What will you give me if I hand Jesus over to you?" So they counted out 30 silver coins for him.

Judas accepted their offer. From then on, Judas watched for the right time to hand Jesus over to them. He wanted to do it when no crowd was around.

Then the day of Unleavened Bread came. That was the time the

Passover lamb had to be sacrificed. Jesus sent Peter and John on ahead. "Go," he told them. "Prepare for us to eat the Passover meal."

"Where do you want us to prepare for it?" they asked.

Jesus replied, "When you enter the city, a man carrying a jar of water will meet you. Follow him to the house he enters. Then say to the owner of the house, 'The Teacher asks, "Where is the guest room? Where can I eat the Passover meal with my disciples?"' He will show you a large upstairs room. It will have furniture and will be ready. Prepare for us to eat there."

The disciples left and went into the city. They found things just as Jesus had told them. So they prepared the Passover meal.

When evening came, Jesus arrived with the Twelve. It was just before the Passover Feast.

When the hour came, Jesus and his apostles took their places at the table. He said to them, "I have really looked forward to eating this Passover meal with you. I wanted to do this before I suffer. I tell you, I will not eat the Passover meal again until it is celebrated in God's kingdom."

After Jesus took the cup, he gave thanks. He said, "Take this cup and share it among yourselves. I tell you, I will not drink wine with you again until God's kingdom comes."

Jesus knew that the time had come for him to leave this world. It was time for him to go to the Father. Jesus loved his disciples who were in the world. So he now showed them how much he really loved them.

The evening meal was being served. The devil had already tempted Judas Iscariot, son of Simon. He had told Judas to hand Jesus over to his enemies.

They also started to argue. They disagreed about which of them was thought to be the most important person.

Jesus said to them, "The kings of the nations hold power over their people. And those who order them around call themselves Protectors. But you must not be like that. Instead, the most important among you should be like the youngest. The one who rules should be like the one who serves.

"Who is more important? Is it the one at the table, or the one who serves? Isn't it the one who is at the table? But I am among you as one who serves. You have stood by me during my troubles. And I give you a kingdom, just as my Father gave me a kingdom. Then you will eat and drink at my table in my kingdom. And you will sit on thrones, judging the 12 tribes of Israel."

Jesus knew that the Father had put everything under his power. He also knew he had come from God and was returning to God.

So he got up from the meal and took off his outer clothes. He wrapped a towel around his waist. After that, he poured water into a large bowl. Then he began to wash his disciples' feet. He dried them with the towel that was wrapped around him.

He came to Simon Peter.

"Lord," Peter said to him, "are you going to wash my feet?"

Jesus replied, "You don't realize now what I am doing. But later you will understand."

"No," said Peter. "You will never wash my feet."

Jesus answered, "Unless I wash you, you can't share life with me."

"Lord," Simon Peter replied, "not just my feet! Wash my hands and my head too!"

Jesus answered, "A person who has had a bath needs to wash only his feet. The rest of his body is clean. And you are clean. But not all of you are."

Jesus knew who was going to hand him over to his enemies. That was why he said not every one was clean.

When Jesus finished washing their feet, he put on his clothes. Then he returned to his place.

"Do you understand what I have done for you?" he asked them. "You call me 'Teacher' and 'Lord.' You are right. That is what I am. I, your Lord and Teacher, have washed your feet. So you also should wash one another's feet. I have given you an example. You should do as I have done for you.

"What I'm about to tell you is true. A servant is not more important than his master. And a messenger is not more important than the one who sends him. Now you know these things. So you will be blessed if you do them.

"I am not talking about all of you. I know those I have chosen. But this will happen so that Scripture will come true. It says, 'The one who shares my bread has deserted me.'[1]

"I am telling you now, before it happens. When it does happen, you will believe that I am he. What I'm about to tell you is true. Anyone who accepts someone I send accepts me. And anyone who accepts me accepts the One who sent me."

After he had said this, Jesus' spirit was troubled. While they were at the table eating, Jesus said, "What I'm about to tell you is true. One of you who is eating with me will hand me over to my enemies. His hand is with mine on the table."

His disciples stared at one another. They had no idea which one of them he meant. The disciples became very sad. One after the other, they began to say to him, "It's not I, Lord, is it?"

"It is one of the Twelve," Jesus replied. "It is the one who dips bread into the bowl with me. The Son of Man will go to his death just as God has already decided. But how terrible it will be for the one who hands him over! It would be better for him if he had not been born."

The apostles began to ask each other about this. They wondered which one of them would do it.

The disciple Jesus loved[2] was next to him at the table. Simon Peter motioned to that disciple. He said, "Ask Jesus which one he means."

The disciple was leaning back against Jesus. He asked him, "Lord, who is it?"

Jesus answered, "It is the one I will give this piece of bread to. I will give it to him after I have dipped it in the dish."

He dipped the piece of bread. Then he gave it to Judas Iscariot, son of Simon. Judas was the one who was going to hand him over. As soon as Judas took the bread, Satan entered into him.

He said, "It's not I, Rabbi, is it?"

Jesus answered, "Yes. It is you."

"Do quickly what you are going to do," Jesus told him.

But no one at the meal understood why Jesus said this to him. Judas was in charge of the money. So some of the disciples thought Jesus was telling him to buy what was needed for the Feast. Others thought Jesus was talking about giving something to poor people.

As soon as Judas had taken the bread, he went out. And it was night.

After Judas was gone, Jesus spoke. He said, "Now the Son of Man receives glory. And he brings glory to God. If the Son brings glory to God, God himself will bring glory to the Son. God will do it at once."

While they were eating, Jesus took bread. He gave thanks and broke it. He handed it to his disciples and said, "Take this and eat it. This is my body. It is given for you. Every time you eat it, do it in memory of me."

In the same way, after the supper he took the cup. He gave thanks and handed it to them. He said, "All of you drink from it. This is my blood of the new covenant. It is poured out to forgive the sins of many. Here is what I tell you. From now on, I won't drink wine with you again until the day I drink it with you in my Father's kingdom."

Then they sang a hymn and went out to the Mount of Olives.

Jesus told them, "This very night you will all turn away because of me. It is written that the Lord said,

"'I will strike the shepherd down.

Then the sheep of the flock will be scattered.'[3]

But after I rise from the dead, I will go ahead of you into Galilee.

181

"My children, I will be with you only a little longer. You will look for me. Just as I told the Jews, so I am telling you now. You can't come where I am going.

"I give you a new command. Love one another. You must love one another, just as I have loved you. If you love one another, everyone will know you are my disciples."

Simon Peter asked him, "Lord, where are you going?"

Jesus replied, "Where I am going you can't follow now. But you will follow me later."

"Lord," Peter asked, "why can't I follow you now? I will give my life for you."

Then Jesus answered, "Will you really give your life for me?"

"Simon, Simon! Satan has asked to sift you disciples like wheat. But I have prayed for you, Simon. I have prayed that your faith will not fail. When you have turned back, help your brothers to be strong."

Peter replied, "All the others may turn away because of you. But I never will."

"What I'm about to tell you is true," Jesus answered. "It will happen this very night. Before the rooster crows, you will say three times that you don't know me."

But Peter would not give in. He said, "I may have to die with you. But I will never say I don't know you." And all the others said the same thing.

Then Jesus asked the disciples, "Did you need anything when I sent you without a purse, bag or sandals?"

"Nothing," they answered.

He said to them, "But now if you have a purse, take it. And also take a bag. If you don't have a sword, sell your coat and buy one. It is written, 'He was counted among those who had committed crimes.'[4] I tell you that what is written about me must come true. Yes, it is already coming true."

The disciples said, "See, Lord, here are two swords."

"That is enough," he replied.

"Do not let your hearts be troubled. Trust in God. Trust in me also.

"There are many rooms in my Father's house. If this were not true, I would have told you. I am going there to prepare a place for you. If I go and do that, I will come back. And I will take you to be with me. Then you will also be where I am.

"You know the way to the place where I am going."

Thomas said to him, "Lord, we don't know where you are going. So how can we know the way?"

Jesus answered, "I am the way and the truth and the life. No one comes to the Father except through me. If you really knew me, you would know my Father also. From now on, you do know him. And you have seen him."

Philip said, "Lord, show us the Father. That will be enough for us."

Jesus answered, "Don't you know me, Philip? I have been among you such a long time! Anyone who has seen me has seen the Father. So how can you say, 'Show us the Father'?

"Don't you believe that I am in the Father? Don't you believe that the Father is in me? The words I say to you are not just my own. The Father lives in me. He is the One who is doing his work. Believe me when I say I am in the Father. Also believe that the Father is in me. Or at least believe what the miracles show about me.

"What I'm about to tell you is true. Anyone who has faith in me will do what I have been doing. In fact, he will do even greater things. That is because I am going to the Father.

"And I will do anything you ask in my name. Then the Son will bring glory to the Father. You may ask me for anything in my name. I will do it.

"If you love me, you will obey what I command. I will ask the Father. And he will give you another Friend to help you and to be with you forever. The Friend is the Spirit of truth. The world can't accept him. That is because the world does not see him or know him. But you know him. He lives with you, and he will be in you.

"I will not leave you like children who don't have parents. I will come to you.

"Before long, the world will not see me anymore. But you will see me. Because I live, you will live also. On that day you will realize that I am in my Father. You will know that you are in me, and I am in you.

"Anyone who has my commands and obeys them loves me. My Father will love the one who loves me. I too will love him. And I will show myself to him."

Then Judas spoke. "Lord," he said, "why do you plan to show yourself only to us? Why not also to the world?" The Judas who spoke those words was not Judas Iscariot.

Jesus replied, "Anyone who loves me will obey my teaching. My Father will love him. We will come to him and make our home with him. Anyone who does not love me will not obey my teaching. The words you hear me say are not my own. They belong to the Father who sent me.

"I have spoken all these things while I am still with you. But the Father will send the Friend in my name to help you. The Friend is the Holy Spirit. He will teach you all things. He will remind you of everything I have said to you.

"I leave my peace with you. I give my peace to you. I do not give it to you as the world does. Do not let your hearts be troubled. And do not be afraid.

"You heard me say, 'I am going away. And I am coming back to you.' If you loved me, you would be glad I am going to the Father. The Father is greater than I am. I have told you now before it happens. Then when it does happen, you will believe.

"I will not speak with you much longer. The prince of this world is coming. He has no power over me. But the world must learn that I love the Father. They must also learn that I do exactly what my Father has commanded me to do.

"Come now. Let us leave.

"I am the true vine. My Father is the gardener. He cuts off every branch joined to me that does not bear fruit. He trims every branch that does bear fruit. Then it will bear even more fruit.

"You are already clean because of the word I have spoken to you. Remain joined to me, and I will remain joined to you. No branch can bear fruit by itself. It must remain joined to the vine. In the same way, you can't bear fruit unless you remain joined to me.

"I am the vine. You are the branches. If anyone remains joined to me, and I to him, he will bear a lot of fruit. You can't do anything without me. If anyone does not remain joined to me, he is like a branch that is thrown away and dries up. Branches like those are picked up. They are thrown into the fire and burned.

"If you remain joined to me and my words remain in you, ask for anything you wish. And it will be given to you. When you bear a lot of fruit, it brings glory to my Father. It shows that you are my disciples.

"Just as the Father has loved me, I have loved you. Now remain in my love. If you obey my commands, you will remain in my love. In the same way, I have obeyed my Father's commands and remain in his love. I have told you this so that my joy will be in you. I also want your joy to be complete.

"Here is my command. Love each other, just as I have loved you. No one has greater love than the one who gives his life for his friends. You are my friends if you do what I command.

"I do not call you servants anymore. Servants do not know their master's business. Instead, I have called you friends. I have told you everything I learned from my Father.

"You did not choose me. Instead, I chose you. I appointed you to go and bear fruit. It is fruit that will last. Then the Father will give you anything you ask for in my name.

"Here is my command. Love each other.

"Does the world hate you? Remember that it hated me first. If you belonged to the world, it would love you like one of its own. But you do not belong to the world. I have chosen you out of the world. That is why the world hates you.

"Remember the words I spoke to you. I said, 'A servant is not more important than his master.' If people hated me and tried to hurt me, they will do the same to you. If they obeyed my teaching, they will obey yours also. They will treat you like that because of my name. They do not know the One who sent me.

"If I had not come and spoken to them, they would not be guilty of sin. But now they have no excuse for their sin. Those who hate me hate my Father also.

"I did miracles among them that no one else did. If I hadn't, they would not be guilty of sin. But now they have seen those miracles. And still they have hated both me and my Father. This has happened so that what is written in their Law would come true. It says, 'They hated me without any reason.'[5]

"I will send the Friend to you from the Father. He is the Spirit of truth, who comes out from the Father. When the Friend comes to help you, he will give witness about me.

"You also must give witness. This is because you have been with me from the beginning.

"I have told you all of this so that you will not go down the wrong path. You will be thrown out of the synagogue. In fact, a time is coming when those who kill you will think they are doing God a favor. They will do things like that because they do not know the Father or me.

"Why have I told you this? So that when the time comes, you will remember that I warned you. I didn't tell you this at first because I was with you.

"Now I am going to the One who sent me. But none of you asks me, 'Where are you going?' Because I have said these things, you are filled with sadness.

"But what I'm about to tell you is true. It is for your good that I am going away. Unless I go away, the Friend will not come to help you. But if I go, I will send him to you. When he comes, he will prove that the world's people are guilty. He will prove their guilt concerning sin and godliness and judgment.

"The world is guilty as far as sin is concerned. That is because people do not believe in me. The world is guilty as far as godliness is concerned. That is because I am going to the Father, where you can't see me anymore. The world is guilty as far as judgment is concerned. That is because the devil, the prince of this world, has already been judged.

"I have much more to say to you. It is more than you can handle right now. But when the Spirit of truth comes, he will guide you into all truth. He will not speak on his own. He will speak only what he hears. And he will tell you what is still going to happen.

"He will bring me glory by receiving something from me and showing it to you. Everything that belongs to the Father is mine. That is why I said the Holy Spirit will receive something from me and show it to you.

"In a little while, you will no longer see me. Then after a little while, you will see me."

Some of his disciples spoke to one another. They said, "What does he mean by saying, 'In a little while, you will no longer see me. Then after a little while, you will see me'? And what does he mean by saying, 'I am going to the Father'?" They kept asking, "What does he mean by 'a little while'? We don't understand what he is saying."

Jesus saw that they wanted to ask him about those things. So he said to them, "Are you asking one another what I meant? Didn't you understand when I said, 'In a little while, you will no longer see me. Then after a little while, you will see me'? What I'm about to tell you is true. You will cry and be full of sorrow while the world is full of joy. You will be sad, but your sadness will turn into joy.

"A woman giving birth to a baby has pain. This is because her time to give birth has come. But when her baby is born, she forgets the pain. She forgets because she is so happy that a baby has been born into the world.

"That's the way it is with you. Now it's your time to be sad. But I will see you again. Then you will be full of joy. And no one will take your joy away.

"When that day comes, you will no longer ask me for anything. What I'm about to tell you is true. My Father will give you anything you ask for in my name. Until now you have not asked for anything in my name. Ask, and you will receive what you ask for. Then your joy will be complete.

"I have not been speaking to you plainly. But a time is coming when I will speak clearly. Then I will tell you plainly about my Father. When that day comes, you will ask for things in my name. I am not saying I will ask the Father instead of you asking him. No, the Father himself loves you because you have loved me. He also loves you because you have believed that I came from God.

"I came from the Father and entered the world. Now I am leaving the world and going back to the Father."

Then Jesus' disciples said, "Now you are speaking plainly. You are using examples that are clear. Now we can see that you know everything. You don't even need anyone to ask you questions. This makes us believe that you came from God."

"At last you believe!" Jesus said. "But a time is coming when you will be scattered and go to your own homes. In fact, that time is already here. You will leave me all alone. But I am not really alone. My Father is with me.

"I have told you these things so that you can have peace because of me. In this world you will have trouble. But cheer up! I have won the battle over the world."

After Jesus said this, he looked toward heaven and prayed. He said, "Father, the time has come. Bring glory to your Son. Then your Son will bring glory to you. You gave him authority over all people. He gives eternal life to all those you have given him.

"And what is eternal life? It is knowing you, the only true God, and Jesus Christ, whom you have sent. I have brought you glory on earth. I have finished the work you gave me to do. So now, Father, give glory to me in heaven where your throne is. Give me the glory I had with you before the world began.

"I have shown you to the disciples you gave me out of the world. They were yours. You gave them to me. And they have obeyed your word. Now they know that everything you have given me comes from you. I gave them the words you gave me. And they accepted them. They knew for certain that I came from you. They believed that you sent me.

"I pray for them. I am not praying for the world. I am praying for those you have given me, because they are yours. All I have is yours, and all you have is mine. Glory has come to me because of my disciples.

"I will not remain in the world any longer. But they are still in the world, and I am coming to you. Holy Father, keep them safe by the power of your name. It is the name you gave me. Keep them safe so they can be one, just as you and I are one.

"While I was with them, I guarded them. I kept them safe through the name you gave me. None of them has been lost, except the one who was sentenced to be destroyed. It happened so that Scripture would come true.

"I am coming to you now. But I say these things while I am still in the world. I say them so that those you gave me can have all my joy inside them. I have given them your word. The world has hated them. This is because they are not part of the world any more than I am. I do not pray that you will take them out of the world. I pray that you will keep them safe from the evil one.

"They do not belong to the world, just as I do not belong to it. Use the truth to make them holy. Your word is truth. You sent me into the world. In the same way, I have sent them into the world. I make myself holy for them so that they too can be made holy in a true sense.

"I do not pray only for them. I pray also for those who will believe in me because of their message. Father, I pray that all of them will be one, just as you are in me and I am in you. I want them also to be in us. Then the world will believe that you have sent me.

"I have given them the glory you gave me. I did this so they would be one, just as we are one. I will be in them, just as you are in me. I want them to be brought together perfectly as one. This will let the world know that you sent me. It will also show the world that you have loved those you gave me, just as you have loved me.

"Father, I want those you have given me to be with me where I am. I want them to see my glory, the glory you have given me. You gave it to me because you loved me before the world was created.

"Father, you are holy. The world does not know you, but I know you. Those you have given me know you have sent me. I have shown you to them. And I will continue to show you to them. Then the love you have for me will be in them. I myself will be in them."

When Jesus had finished praying, he left with his disciples. Then Jesus went with his disciples to a place called Gethsemane. They crossed the Kidron Valley. On the other side there was a grove of olive trees. Jesus and his disciples went into it.

Judas knew the place. He was going to hand Jesus over to his enemies. Jesus had often met in that place with his disciples.

Jesus said to them, "Sit here while I pray."

He took Peter, James and John along with him. He began to be very upset and troubled. Then he said to them, "My soul is very sad. I feel close to death. Stay here. Keep watch with me. Pray that you won't fall into sin when you are tempted."

He went a little farther. Then he fell with his face to the ground. He prayed that, if possible, the hour might pass by him. "Abba,"[6] he said, "everything is possible for you. Take this cup of suffering away from me. But let what you want be done, not what I want."

An angel from heaven appeared to Jesus and gave him strength. Because he was very sad and troubled, he prayed even harder. His sweat was like drops of blood falling to the ground.

After that, he got up from prayer and went back to the disciples.

He found them sleeping. They were worn out because they were very sad.

"Simon," he said to Peter, "are you asleep? Couldn't you keep watch for one hour? Watch and pray. Then you won't fall into sin when you are tempted. The spirit is willing. But the body is weak."

Jesus went away a second time. He prayed, "My Father, is it possible for this cup to be taken away? But if I must drink it, may what you want be done."

Then he came back. Again he found them sleeping. They couldn't keep their eyes open.

"Why are you sleeping?" he asked them. "Get up! Pray that you won't fall into sin when you are tempted."

They did not know what to say to him. So he left them and went away once more. For the third time he prayed the same thing.

Jesus returned the third time. He said to them, "Are you still sleeping and resting? Enough! The hour has come. Look! The Son of Man is about to be handed over to sinners. Get up! Let us go! Here comes the one who is handing me over to them!"

While Jesus was still speaking, Judas arrived. He was guiding a group of soldiers and some officials. A crowd was with him. They were carrying swords and clubs. The chief priests, the teachers of the law, and the elders had sent them.

Judas, who was going to hand Jesus over, had arranged a signal with them. "The one I kiss is the man," he said. "Arrest him and have the guards lead him away."

Judas approached Jesus to kiss him. But Jesus asked him, "Judas, are you handing over the Son of Man with a kiss?"

So Judas went to Jesus at once. He said, "Greetings, Rabbi!" And he kissed him.

Jesus replied, "Friend, do what you came to do."

Jesus knew everything that was going to happen to him. So he went out and asked them, "Who is it that you want?"

"Jesus of Nazareth," they replied.

"I am he," Jesus said.

Judas, who was going to hand Jesus over, was standing there with them. When Jesus said, "I am he," they moved back. Then they fell to the ground.

He asked them again, "Who is it that you want?"

They said, "Jesus of Nazareth."

"I told you I am he," Jesus answered. "If you are looking for me, then let these men go." This happened so that the words Jesus had spoken would come true. He had said, "I have not lost anyone God has given me."

Then the men stepped forward. They grabbed Jesus and arrested him.

Jesus' followers saw what was going to happen. So they said, "Lord, should we use our swords against them?"

Simon Peter had a sword and pulled it out. He struck the high priest's servant and cut off his right ear. The servant's name was Malchus.

Jesus commanded Peter, "Put your sword away! All who use the sword will die by the sword. Do you think I can't ask my Father for help? He would send an army of more than 70,000 angels right away. But then how would the Scriptures come true? They say it must happen in this way. Shouldn't I drink the cup of suffering the Father has given me?"

And he touched the man's ear and healed him.

Then Jesus spoke to the chief priests, the officers of the temple guard, and the elders. They had all come for him. "Am I leading a band of armed men against you?" he asked. "Do you have to come with swords and clubs? Every day I was with you in the temple courtyard. And you didn't lay a hand on me. But this is your hour. This is when darkness rules. All this has happened so that the words of the prophets would come true."

Then the group of soldiers, their leader and the Jewish officials arrested Jesus. All the disciples left him and ran away.

A young man[7] was following Jesus. The man was wearing nothing but a piece of linen cloth. When the crowd grabbed him, he ran away naked. He left his clothing behind.

chapter eighteen

Facing False Charges

T hose who had arrested Jesus took him to Caiaphas, the high
priest. All of the chief priests, the elders, and the teachers
of the law came together. They tied him up and brought him
first to Annas. He was the father-in-law of Caiaphas, the high priest
at that time. Caiaphas had advised the Jews that it would be good if
one man died for the people.

Simon Peter and another disciple were following Jesus. The high
priest knew the other disciple. So that disciple went with Jesus
into the high priest's courtyard. But Peter had to wait outside by
the door.

The other disciple came back. He was the one the high priest
knew. He spoke to the woman who was on duty there. Then he
brought Peter in.

The woman at the door spoke to Peter. "You are not one of Jesus'
disciples, are you?" she asked him.

"I am not," he replied.

It was cold. The servants and officials stood around a fire. They
had made it to keep warm. Peter was also standing with them. He
warmed himself at the fire. Then they sat down together. Peter sat
down with them.

Meanwhile, Annas questioned Jesus. He asked him about his disciples and his teaching.

"I have spoken openly to the world," Jesus replied. "I always taught in synagogues or at the temple, where all the Jews come together. I didn't say anything in secret. Why question me? Ask the people who heard me. They certainly know what I said."

When Jesus said that, one of the officials nearby hit him in the face. "Is this any way to answer the high priest?" he asked.

"Have I said something wrong?" Jesus replied. "If I have, give witness to it. But if I spoke the truth, why did you hit me?"

While Jesus was still tied up, Annas sent him to Caiaphas, the high priest.

The chief priests and the whole Sanhedrin were looking for something to use against Jesus. They wanted to put him to death. But they did not find any proof, even though many false witnesses came forward. Many witnesses lied about him. But their stories did not agree.

Finally, two other witnesses came forward. They said, "This fellow claimed, 'I am able to destroy the temple of God. I can build it again in three days.' We heard him say, 'I will destroy this temple made by human hands. In three days I will build another temple, not made by human hands.'" But what they said did not agree.

Then the high priest stood up in front of them. He asked Jesus, "Aren't you going to answer? What are these charges these men are bringing against you?"

But Jesus remained silent. He gave no answer.

The high priest said to him, "I command you under oath by the living God. Tell us if you are the Christ, the Son of God."

"Yes. It is just as you say," Jesus replied.

Again the high priest asked him, "Are you the Christ? Are you the Son of the Blessed One?"

"I am," said Jesus. "But here is what I say to all of you. In days to come, you will see the Son of Man sitting at the right hand of the Mighty One. You will see the Son of Man coming on the clouds of heaven."

Then the high priest tore his clothes. He said, "He has spoken a very evil thing against God! Why do we need any more witnesses? You have heard him say this evil thing. What do you think?"

"He must die!" they answered. They all found him guilty and said he must die.

There were men guarding Jesus. They began laughing at him and beating him. Then they spit in his face. They blindfolded him. They hit him with their fists. Others slapped him. They said, "Prophesy to us, Christ! Who hit you?" They also said many other things to make fun of him.

Peter was below in the courtyard. One of the high priest's female servants came by. When she saw Peter warming himself, she looked closely at him.

"You also were with Jesus of Galilee," she said.

But in front of all of them, Peter said he was not. "I don't know what you're talking about," he said.

Then he went out to the gate leading into the courtyard. There another woman saw him. She said to the people, "This fellow was with Jesus of Nazareth."

Again he said he was not. With an oath he said, "I don't know the man!"

After a little while, those standing nearby said to Peter, "You must be one of them. You are from Galilee. The way you talk gives you away."

One of the high priest's servants was a relative of the man whose ear Peter had cut off. He said to Peter, "Didn't I see you with Jesus in the olive grove?"

Peter replied, "Man, I don't know what you're talking about!"

Then Peter began to call down curses on himself. He took an oath and said to them, "I don't know the man!"

Just as he was speaking, the rooster crowed. The Lord turned and looked right at Peter. Then Peter remembered what the Lord had spoken to him. "The rooster will crow today," Jesus had said.

"Before it does, you will say three times that you don't know me."
Peter went outside. He broke down and sobbed.

At dawn the elders of the people met together. These included the
chief priests and the teachers of the law. Jesus was led to them. "If
you are the Christ," they said, "tell us."

Jesus answered, "If I tell you, you will not believe me. And if I
asked you, you would not answer. But from now on, the Son of Man
will be seated at the right hand of the mighty God."

They all asked, "Are you the Son of God then?"

He replied, "You are right in saying that I am."

Then they said, "Why do we need any more witnesses? We have
heard it from his own lips."

All the chief priests and the elders of the people decided to put
Jesus to death. They tied him up and led him away.

Judas, who had handed him over, saw that Jesus had been sentenced to die. He felt deep shame and sadness for what he had
done. So he returned the 30 silver coins to the chief priests and
the elders. "I have sinned," he said. "I handed over a man who is
not guilty."

"What do we care?" they replied. "That's your problem."

So Judas threw the money into the temple and left. Then he
went away and hanged himself.

The chief priests picked up the coins. They said, "It's against the
law to put this money into the temple fund. It is blood money. It
has paid for a man's death." So they decided to use the money to
buy a potter's field. People from other countries would be buried
there. That is why it has been called The Field of Blood to this very
day. Then the words spoken by Jeremiah the prophet came true. He
said, "They took the 30 silver coins. That price was set for him
by the people of Israel. They used the coins to buy a potter's field,
just as the Lord commanded me."[1]

The Jews led Jesus from Caiaphas to the palace of the Roman
governor. Then they handed him over to Pilate, who was the

Governor. By now it was early morning. The Jews did not want to be made "unclean." They wanted to be able to eat the Passover meal. So they did not enter the palace.

Pilate came out to them. He asked, "What charges are you bringing against this man?"

"He has committed crimes," they replied. "If he hadn't, we would not have handed him over to you."

Pilate said, "Take him yourselves. Judge him by your own law."

"But we don't have the right to put anyone to death," the Jews complained. This happened so that the words Jesus had spoken about how he was going to die would come true.

They began to bring charges against Jesus. They said, "We have found this man misleading our people. He is against paying taxes to Caesar. And he claims to be Christ, a king."[2]

So Pilate asked Jesus, "Are you the king of the Jews?"

"Yes. It is just as you say," Jesus replied.

But when the chief priests and the elders brought charges against him he did not answer. So Pilate asked him again, "Aren't you going to answer? See how many things they charge you with. Don't you hear the charges they are bringing against you?"

But Jesus made no reply, not even to a single charge. The governor was really amazed.

Then Pilate went back inside the palace. He ordered Jesus to be brought to him. Pilate asked him, "Are you the king of the Jews?"

"Is that your own idea?" Jesus asked. "Or did others talk to you about me?"

"Am I a Jew?" Pilate replied. "It was your people and your chief priests who handed you over to me. What have you done?"

Jesus said, "My kingdom is not part of this world. If it were, those who serve me would fight. They would try to keep the Jews from arresting me. My kingdom is from another place."

"So you are a king, then!" said Pilate.

Jesus answered, "You are right to say I am a king. In fact, that's the reason I was born. I came into the world to give witness to the truth. Everyone who is on the side of truth listens to me."

"What is truth?" Pilate asked.

Then Pilate went out again to the Jews. He announced, "I find no basis for a charge against this man."

But they kept it up. They said, "His teaching stirs up the people all over Judea. He started in Galilee and has come all the way here."

When Pilate heard this, he asked if the man was from Galilee. He learned that Jesus was from Herod's area of authority. So Pilate sent Jesus to Herod. At that time Herod was also in Jerusalem.

When Herod saw Jesus, he was very pleased. He had been wanting to see Jesus for a long time. He had heard much about him. He hoped to see Jesus do a miracle.

Herod asked him many questions, but Jesus gave him no answer. The chief priests and the teachers of the law were standing there. With loud shouts they brought charges against him.

Herod and his soldiers laughed at him and made fun of him. They dressed him in a beautiful robe. Then they sent him back to Pilate. That day Herod and Pilate became friends. Before this time they had been enemies.

Pilate called together the chief priests, the rulers and the people. He said to them, "You brought me this man. You said he was turning the people against the authorities. I have questioned him in front of you. I have found no basis for your charges against him. Herod hasn't either. So he sent Jesus back to us. As you can see, Jesus has done nothing that is worthy of death. So I will just have him whipped and let him go."

It was the governor's practice at the Passover Feast to let one prisoner go free. The people could choose the one they wanted. At that time they had a well-known prisoner named Barabbas. He was there with some other people who had fought against the country's rulers. They had committed murder while they were fighting against the rulers.

The crowd came up and asked Pilate to do for them what he usually did. So when the crowd gathered, Pilate asked them, "Which one do you want me to set free? Barabbas? Or Jesus who is called Christ?"

Pilate knew that the leaders were jealous. He knew this was why they had handed Jesus over to him.

While Pilate was sitting on the judge's seat, his wife sent him a message. It said, "Don't have anything to do with that man. He is not guilty. I have suffered a great deal in a dream today because of him."

But the chief priests and the elders talked the crowd into asking for Barabbas and having Jesus put to death.

"Which of the two do you want me to set free?" asked the governor. "Do you want me to let the king of the Jews go free?"

"Barabbas," they answered.

"Then what should I do with Jesus who is called Christ?" Pilate asked.

With one voice the crowd cried out, "Kill this man! Give Barabbas to us!"

Pilate wanted to let Jesus go. So he made an appeal to the crowd again. "Then what should I do with the one you call the king of the Jews?" Pilate asked them.

"But they kept shouting, "Crucify him! Crucify him!"

Pilate spoke to them for the third time. "Why?" he asked. "What wrong has this man done? I have found no reason to have him put to death. So I will just have him whipped and let him go."

But they shouted even louder, "Crucify him!"

Then Pilate took Jesus and had him whipped. [3] The soldiers twisted thorns together to make a crown. They put it on Jesus' head. Then they put a purple robe on him. They went up to him again and again. They kept saying, "We honor you, king of the Jews!" And they hit him in the face.

Once more Pilate came out. He said to the Jews, "Look, I am

bringing Jesus out to you. I want to let you know that I find no basis for a charge against him."

Jesus came out wearing the crown of thorns and the purple robe. Then Pilate said to them, "Here is the man!"

As soon as the chief priests and their officials saw him, they shouted, "Crucify him! Crucify him!"

But Pilate answered, "You take him and crucify him. I myself find no basis for a charge against him."

The Jews replied, "We have a law. That law says he must die. He claimed to be the Son of God."

When Pilate heard that, he was even more afraid. He went back inside the palace. "Where do you come from?" he asked Jesus.

But Jesus did not answer him.

"Do you refuse to speak to me?" Pilate said. "Don't you understand? I have the power to set you free or to nail you to a cross."

Jesus answered, "You were given power from heaven. If you weren't, you would have no power over me. So the one who handed me over to you is guilty of a greater sin."

From then on, Pilate tried to set Jesus free. But the Jews kept shouting, "If you let this man go, you are not Caesar's friend! Anyone who claims to be a king is against Caesar!"

When Pilate heard that, he brought Jesus out. Pilate sat down on the judge's seat. It was at a place called The Stone Walkway. In the Aramaic language it was called Gabbatha.

"Here is your king," Pilate said to the Jews.

But they shouted, "Kill him! Kill him! Crucify him!"

"Should I crucify your king?" Pilate asked.

"We have no king but Caesar," the chief priests answered.

Pilate saw that he wasn't getting anywhere. Instead, the crowd was starting to get angry. So he took water and washed his hands in front of them. "I am not guilty of this man's death," he said. "You are accountable for that!"

All the people answered, "We and our children will accept the guilt for his death!"

With loud shouts they kept calling for Jesus to be crucified. The people's shouts won out.

Pilate wanted to satisfy the crowd. So Pilate decided to give them what they wanted. He set free the man they asked for.

Finally, Pilate handed Jesus over to them to be nailed to a cross.

chapter nineteen

Nailed to a Cross

The governor's soldiers took Jesus into the palace, which was called the Praetorium. All the rest of the soldiers gathered around him. They took off his clothes and put a purple robe on him. Then they twisted thorns together to make a crown. They placed it on his head. They put a stick in his right hand. Then they fell on their knees in front of him and made fun of him. "We honor you, king of the Jews!" they said. They spit on him. They hit him on the head with the stick again and again. They fell on their knees and pretended to honor him.

After they had made fun of him, they took off the robe. They put his own clothes back on him. Then they led him away to nail him to a cross. He had to carry his own cross.

They went out to a place called The Skull. In the Aramaic language it was called Golgotha. On their way out of the city, they met a man from Cyrene. His name was Simon. He was the father of Alexander and Rufus. Simon was on his way in from the country. The soldiers forced him to carry the cross.

A large number of people followed Jesus. Some were women whose hearts were filled with sorrow. They cried loudly because of him.

Jesus turned and said to them, "Daughters of Jerusalem, do not cry for me. Cry for yourselves and for your children. The time will come when you will say, 'Blessed are the women who can't have

children! Blessed are those who never gave birth or nursed babies!'
It is written,

"'The people will say to the mountains, "Fall on us!"

They'll say to the hills, "Cover us!"'[1]

People do these things when trees are green. So what will happen
when trees are dry?"

Two other men were also led out with Jesus to be killed. Both of
them had broken the law.

The soldiers brought them to the place called The Skull. Then they
gave him wine mixed with spices.[2] After tasting it, he refused to
drink it.

There they nailed Jesus to the cross. Jesus said, "Father, forgive
them. They don't know what they are doing."

It was nine o'clock in the morning when they crucified him.
They crucified two robbers with him. One was on his right and
one was on his left.

When they had nailed him to the cross, they divided his clothes
by casting lots. They divided them into four parts. Each soldier got
one part. Jesus' long, inner robe was left. It did not have any seams.
It was made out of one piece of cloth from top to bottom.

"Let's not tear it," they said to one another. "Let's cast lots to see
who will get it."

This happened so that Scripture would come true. It says,

"They divided up my clothes among them.

They cast lots for what I was wearing."[3]

So that is what the soldiers did. They sat down and kept watch over
him there.

Pilate had a notice prepared. Above his head they placed the
written charge against him. It was fastened to the cross. It read,
JESUS OF NAZARETH, KING OF THE JEWS. Many of the Jews read the
sign. The place where Jesus was crucified was near the city. The sign
was written in the Aramaic, Latin and Greek languages.[4]

The chief priests of the Jews argued with Pilate. They said, "Do not write 'The King of the Jews.' Write that this man claimed to be king of the Jews."

Pilate answered, "I have written what I have written."

The people stood there watching. Those who passed by shouted at Jesus and made fun of him. They shook their heads and said, "So you are going to destroy the temple and build it again in three days? Then save yourself! Come down from the cross, if you are the Son of God!"

In the same way the chief priests, the teachers of the law and the elders made fun of him. "He saved others," they said. "But he can't save himself! Let this Christ, this King of Israel, come down now from the cross! When we see that, we will believe. He trusts in God. Let God rescue him now if he wants him. He's the one who said, 'I am the Son of God.'"

The soldiers also came up and poked fun at him. They offered him wine vinegar. They said, "If you are the king of the Jews, save yourself."

One of the criminals hanging there made fun of Jesus. He said, "Aren't you the Christ? Save yourself! Save us!"

But the other criminal scolded him. "Don't you have any respect for God?" he said. "Remember, you are under the same sentence of death. We are being punished fairly. We are getting just what our actions call for. But this man hasn't done anything wrong."

Then he said, "Jesus, remember me when you come into your kingdom."

Jesus answered him, "What I'm about to tell you is true. Today you will be with me in paradise."

Jesus' mother stood near his cross. So did his mother's sister, Mary the wife of Clopas, and Mary Magdalene.

Jesus saw his mother there. He also saw the disciple he loved standing nearby. Jesus said to his mother, "Dear woman, here is your son." He said to the disciple, "Here is your mother." From that time on, the disciple took her into his home.

It was now about noon. The whole land was covered with darkness until three o'clock. The sun had stopped shining. About three o'clock, Jesus cried out in a loud voice. He said, "Eloi, Eloi, lama sabachthani?" This means "My God, my God, why have you deserted me?"[5]

Some of those standing nearby heard Jesus cry out. They said, "Listen! He's calling for Elijah."

Later Jesus said, "I am thirsty." He knew that everything was now finished. He knew that what Scripture said must come true.

A jar of wine vinegar was there. Right away one of them ran and got a sponge. He filled it with wine vinegar and put it on a stick. He offered it to Jesus to drink. The rest said, "Leave him alone. Let's see if Elijah comes to save him."

After Jesus drank he said, "It is finished."

Jesus called out in a loud voice, "Father, into your hands I commit my very life." After he said this, he took his last breath. Then he bowed his head and died.

At that moment the temple curtain[6] was torn in two from top to bottom. The earth shook. The rocks split. Tombs broke open. The bodies of many holy people who had died were raised to life. They came out of the tombs. After Jesus was raised to life, they went into the holy city. There they appeared to many people.

The Roman commander and those guarding Jesus saw the earthquake and all that had happened. They were terrified.

The Roman commander was standing there in front of Jesus. He heard his cry and saw how Jesus died. Then he said, "This man was surely the Son of God!" He praised God and said, "Jesus was surely a man who did what was right."

The people had gathered to watch that sight. When they saw what happened, they beat their chests and went away. But all those who knew Jesus stood not very far away, watching those things. They included the women who had followed him from Galilee.

Mary Magdalene was among them. Mary, the mother of the younger James and of Joses, was also there. So was Salome. In Galilee those women had followed Jesus. They had taken care of his needs. Many other women were also there. They had come up with him to Jerusalem.

It was Preparation Day. The next day would be a special Sabbath. The Jews did not want the bodies left on the crosses during the Sabbath. So they asked Pilate to have the legs broken[7] and the bodies taken down. The soldiers came and broke the legs of the first man who had been crucified with Jesus. Then they broke the legs of the other man.

But when they came to Jesus, they saw that he was already dead. So they did not break his legs. Instead, one of the soldiers stuck his spear into Jesus' side. Right away, blood and water flowed out. The man who saw it has given witness. And his witness is true. He knows that he tells the truth. He gives witness so that you also can believe.

These things happened in order that Scripture would come true. It says, "Not one of his bones will be broken." Scripture also says, "They will look to the one they have pierced."[8]

As evening approached, a rich man came from the town of Arimathea. His name was Joseph. He was a leading member of the Jewish Council. He was waiting for God's kingdom. He was a good and honest man. He had not agreed with what the leaders had decided and done. He was a follower of Jesus. But he followed Jesus secretly because he was afraid of the Jews.

Joseph went boldly to Pilate and asked for Jesus' body. Pilate was surprised to hear that Jesus was already dead. So he called for the Roman commander. He asked him if Jesus had already died. The commander said it was true. So Pilate gave the body to Joseph.

After Pilate gave him permission, Joseph came and took the body away.

Nicodemus went with Joseph. He was the man who had earlier visited Jesus at night. Nicodemus brought some mixed spices, about 75 pounds. The two men took Jesus' body. They wrapped it in strips of linen cloth, along with the spices. That was the way the Jews buried people's bodies.

At the place where Jesus was crucified, there was a garden. A new tomb was there. No one had ever been put in it before.

That day was the Jewish Preparation Day and the tomb was nearby. The Sabbath was about to begin. So they placed Jesus there. Joseph took the body and wrapped it in a clean linen cloth. He placed it in his own new tomb that he had cut out of the rock. He rolled a big stone in front of the entrance to the tomb. Then he went away.

The women who had come with Jesus from Galilee followed Joseph. Mary Magdalene and the other Mary were sitting there across from the tomb. They saw the tomb and how Jesus' body was placed in it.

Then they went home. There they prepared spices and perfumes. But they rested on the Sabbath day in order to obey the Law.

The next day was the day after Preparation Day. The chief priests and the Pharisees went to Pilate. "Sir," they said, "we remember something that liar said while he was still alive. He claimed, 'After three days I will rise again.' So give the order to make the tomb secure until the third day. If you don't, his disciples might come and steal the body. Then they will tell the people that Jesus has been raised from the dead. This last lie will be worse than the first."

"Take some guards with you," Pilate answered. "Go. Make the tomb as secure as you can." So they went and made the tomb secure. They put a seal on the stone and placed some guards on duty.

chapter twenty

Back From the Dead

The Sabbath day was now over. It was dawn on the first day of the week. Mary Magdalene and the other Mary went to look at the tomb.

There was a powerful earthquake. An angel of the Lord came down from heaven. The angel went to the tomb. He rolled back the stone and sat on it. His body shone like lightning. His clothes were as white as snow. The guards were so afraid of him that they shook and became like dead men.

Mary Magdalene, Mary the mother of James, and Salome bought spices. The women took the spices they had prepared. They were going to apply them to Jesus' body.

Very early on the first day of the week, they were on their way to the tomb. It was just after sunrise. They asked each other, "Who will roll the stone away from the entrance to the tomb?"

Then they looked up and saw that the stone had been rolled away. The stone was very large.

When they entered the tomb, they did not find the body of the Lord Jesus. They were wondering about this.

Suddenly two men in clothes as bright as lightning stood beside them. The women were terrified. They bowed down with their faces to the ground. As they did, they saw a young man dressed in a white robe. He was sitting on the right side.

The angel said to the women, "Don't be afraid. I know that you are looking for Jesus, who was crucified. He is not here! He has risen, just as he said he would! Come and see the place where he was lying."

Then the men said to them, "Why do you look for the living among the dead? Remember how he told you he would rise. It was while he was still with you in Galilee. He said, 'The Son of Man must be handed over to sinful people. He must be nailed to a cross. On the third day he will rise from the dead.' Go quickly! Tell his disciples, 'He has risen from the dead. He is going ahead of you into Galilee. There you will see him. It will be just as he told you.'"

Then the women remembered Jesus' words. The women were shaking and confused. They went out and ran away from the tomb. They said nothing to anyone, because they were afraid.

They came back from the tomb. They told all these things to the Eleven and to all the others. Mary Magdalene, Joanna, Mary the mother of James, and the others with them were the ones who told the apostles.

Mary Magdalene ran to Simon Peter and another disciple, the one Jesus loved. She said, "They have taken the Lord out of the tomb! We don't know where they have put him!"

But the apostles did not believe the women. Their words didn't make any sense to them.

So Peter and the other disciple started out for the tomb. Both of them were running. The other disciple ran faster than Peter. He reached the tomb first. He bent over and looked in at the strips of linen lying there. But he did not go in.

Then Simon Peter, who was behind him, arrived. He went into the tomb. He saw the strips of linen lying there. He also saw the burial cloth that had been around Jesus' head. The cloth was folded up by itself. It was separate from the linen. Then he went away, wondering what had happened.

The disciple who had reached the tomb first also went inside. He saw and believed. They still did not understand from Scripture that Jesus had to rise from the dead. Then the disciples went back to their homes. But Mary stood outside the tomb crying.

Jesus rose from the dead early on the first day of the week. He appeared first to Mary Magdalene. He had driven seven demons out of her.

As she cried, she bent over to look into the tomb. She saw two angels dressed in white. They were seated where Jesus' body had been. One of them was where Jesus' head had been laid. The other sat where his feet had been placed.

They asked her, "Woman, why are you crying?"

"They have taken my Lord away," she said. "I don't know where they have put him."

Then she turned around and saw Jesus standing there. But she didn't realize that it was Jesus.

"Woman," he said, "why are you crying? Who are you looking for?"

She thought he was the gardener. So she said, "Sir, did you carry him away? Tell me where you put him. Then I will go and get him."

Jesus said to her, "Mary."

She turned toward him. Then she cried out in the Aramaic language, "Rabboni!" Rabboni means Teacher.

Jesus said, "Do not hold on to me. I have not yet returned to the Father. Instead, go to those who believe in me. Tell them, 'I am returning to my Father and your Father, to my God and your God.'"

So the women hurried away from the tomb. They were afraid, but they were filled with joy. They ran to tell the disciples.

Suddenly Jesus met them. "Greetings!" he said.

They came to him, took hold of his feet and worshiped him.

Then Jesus said to them, "Don't be afraid. Go and tell my brothers to go to Galilee. There they will see me."

Mary Magdalene went to the disciples with the news. She went and told those who had been with him. She found them crying. They were very sad. She said, "I have seen the Lord!" And she told them that he had said these things to her. They heard that Jesus was alive and that she had seen him. But they did not believe it.

While the women were on their way, some of the guards went into the city. They reported to the chief priests all that had happened.

When the chief priests met with the elders, they came up with a plan. They gave the soldiers a large amount of money. They told the soldiers, "We want you to say, 'His disciples came during the night. They stole his body while we were sleeping.' If the governor hears this report, we will pay him off. That will keep you out of trouble."

So the soldiers took the money and did as they were told. This story has spread all around among the Jews to this very day.

After that, Jesus appeared in a different form to two of them. That same day, two of Jesus' followers were going to a village called Emmaus. It was about seven miles from Jerusalem. They were talking with each other about everything that had happened.

As they talked about those things, Jesus himself came up and walked along with them. But God kept them from recognizing him.

Jesus asked them, "What are you talking about as you walk along?"

They stood still, and their faces were sad. One of them was named Cleopas. He said to Jesus, "You must be a visitor to Jerusalem. If you lived there, you would know the things that have happened there in the last few days."

"What things?" Jesus asked.

"About Jesus of Nazareth," they replied. "He was a prophet. He was powerful in what he said and did in the eyes of God and all of the people. The chief priests and our rulers handed Jesus over to be sentenced to death. They nailed him to a cross. But we had hoped that he was the one who was going to set Israel free. Also, it is the third day since all this happened.

"Some of our women amazed us too. Early this morning they

went to the tomb. But they didn't find his body. So they came and told us what they had seen. They saw angels, who said Jesus was alive. Then some of our friends went to the tomb. They saw it was empty, just as the women had said. They didn't see Jesus' body there."

Jesus said to them, "How foolish you are! How long it takes you to believe all that the prophets said! Didn't the Christ have to suffer these things and then receive his glory?"

Jesus explained to them what was said about himself in all the Scriptures. He began with Moses and all the Prophets.

The two men approached the village where they were going. Jesus acted as if he were going farther. But they tried hard to keep him from leaving. They said, "Stay with us. It is nearly evening. The day is almost over." So he went in to stay with them.

He joined them at the table. Then he took bread and gave thanks. He broke it and began to give it to them. Their eyes were opened, and they recognized him. But then he disappeared from their sight.

They said to each other, "He talked with us on the road. He opened the Scriptures to us. Weren't our hearts burning inside us during that time?"

They got up and returned at once to Jerusalem. There they found the Eleven and those with them. They were all gathered together. They were saying, "It's true! The Lord has risen! He has appeared to Simon!"

Then the two of them told what had happened to them on the way. They told how they had recognized Jesus when he broke the bread.

On the evening of that first day of the week, the disciples were together. They had locked the doors because they were afraid of the Jews.

The disciples were still talking about this when Jesus himself suddenly stood among them. He said, "May peace be with you!"

They were surprised and terrified. They thought they were seeing a ghost.

Jesus said to them, "Why are you troubled? Why do you have doubts in your minds? Look at my hands and my feet. It is really I! Touch me and see. A ghost does not have a body or bones. But you can see that I do."

After he said that, he showed them his hands and feet. But they still did not believe it. They were amazed and filled with joy.

So Jesus asked them, "Do you have anything here to eat?"

They gave him a piece of cooked fish. He took it and ate it in front of them.

He spoke firmly to them because they had no faith. They would not believe those who had seen him after he rose from the dead.

Thomas was one of the Twelve. He was called Didymus.[1] He was not with the other disciples when Jesus came. So they told him, "We have seen the Lord!"

But he said to them, "First I must see the nail marks in his hands. I must put my finger where the nails were. I must put my hand into his side. Only then will I believe what you say."

A week later, Jesus' disciples were in the house again. Thomas was with them. Even though the doors were locked, Jesus came in and stood among them.

He said, "May peace be with you!" Then he said to Thomas, "Put your finger here. See my hands. Reach out your hand and put it into my side. Stop doubting and believe."

Thomas said to him, "My Lord and my God!"

Then Jesus told him, "Because you have seen me, you have believed. Blessed are those who have not seen me but still have believed."

chapter twenty-one

More to Come

Before Jesus left, he gave orders to the apostles he had chosen. He did this through the Holy Spirit. After his suffering and death, he appeared to them. In many ways he proved that he was alive. He appeared to them over a period of 40 days. During that time he spoke about God's kingdom.[1]

The 11 disciples went to Galilee. They went to the mountain where Jesus had told them to go. When they saw him, they worshiped him. But some still had their doubts.

Then Jesus came to them. He said, "All authority in heaven and on earth has been given to me. So you must go and make disciples of all nations. Baptize them in the name of the Father and of the Son and of the Holy Spirit. Teach them to obey everything I have commanded you. And you can be sure that I am always with you, to the very end."

Again Jesus said, "May peace be with you! The Father has sent me. So now I am sending you." He then breathed on them. He said, "Receive the Holy Spirit. If you forgive anyone's sins, they are forgiven. If you do not forgive them, they are not forgiven."

He said to them, "Go into all the world. Preach the good news to everyone. Anyone who believes and is baptized will be saved. But anyone who does not believe will be punished. Here are the miraculous signs that those who believe will do. In my name they will drive out demons. They will speak in languages they had not known before. They will pick up snakes with their hands. And when they drink deadly poison, it will not hurt them at all. They will place their hands on sick people. And the people will get well."

After this, Jesus appeared to his disciples again. It was by the Sea of Galilee. Here is what happened.

Simon Peter and Thomas, who was called Didymus, were there together. Nathanael from Cana in Galilee and James and John, the sons of Zebedee, were with them. So were two other disciples.

"I'm going out to fish," Simon Peter told them. They said, "We'll go with you." So they went out and got into the boat. That night they didn't catch anything.

Early in the morning, Jesus stood on the shore. But the disciples did not realize that it was Jesus.

He called out to them, "Friends, don't you have any fish?"

"No," they answered.

He said, "Throw your net on the right side of the boat. There you will find some fish."

When they did, they could not pull the net into the boat. There were too many fish in it.

Then the disciple Jesus loved said to Simon Peter, "It is the Lord!"

As soon as Peter heard that, he put his coat on. He had taken it off earlier. Then he jumped into the water.

The other disciples followed in the boat. They were towing the net full of fish. The shore was only about 100 yards away. When they landed, they saw a fire of burning coals. There were fish on it. There was also some bread.

Jesus said to them, "Bring some of the fish you have just caught."

Simon Peter climbed into the boat. He dragged the net to shore. It was full of large fish. There were 153 of them. But even with that many fish the net was not torn.

Jesus said to them, "Come and have breakfast."

None of the disciples dared to ask him, "Who are you?" They knew it was the Lord.

Jesus came, took the bread and gave it to them. He did the same thing with the fish. This was the third time Jesus appeared to his disciples after he was raised from the dead.

When Jesus and the disciples had finished eating, Jesus spoke to Simon Peter. He asked, "Simon, son of John, do you really love me more than these others do?"

"Yes, Lord," he answered. "You know that I love you."

Jesus said, "Feed my lambs."

Again Jesus asked, "Simon, son of John, do you really love me?"

He answered, "Yes, Lord. You know that I love you."

Jesus said, "Take care of my sheep."

Jesus spoke to him a third time. He asked, "Simon, son of John, do you love me?"

Peter felt bad because Jesus asked him the third time, "Do you love me?" He answered, "Lord, you know all things. You know that I love you."

Jesus said, "Feed my sheep. What I'm about to tell you is true. When you were younger, you dressed yourself. You went wherever you wanted to go. But when you are old, you will stretch out your hands. Someone else will dress you. Someone else will lead you where you do not want to go."

Jesus said this to point out how Peter would die. His death would bring glory to God.

Then Jesus said to him, "Follow me!"

Peter turned around. He saw that the disciple Jesus loved was following them. He was the one who had leaned back against Jesus at the supper. He had said, "Lord, who is going to hand you over to your enemies?" When Peter saw that disciple, he asked, "Lord, what will happen to him?"

Jesus answered, "Suppose I want him to remain alive until I return. What does that matter to you? You must follow me."

Because of what Jesus said, a false report spread among the believers. The story was told that the disciple Jesus loved wouldn't die. But Jesus did not say he would not die. He only said, "Suppose I want him to remain alive until I return. What does that matter to you?"

This is the disciple who gives witness to these things. He also wrote them down. We know that his witness is true. [2]

One day Jesus was eating with them. He gave them a command. "Do not leave Jerusalem," he said. "Wait for the gift my Father promised. You have heard me talk about it. John baptized with water. But in a few days you will be baptized with the Holy Spirit."

Jesus said to them, "This is what I told you while I was still with you. Everything written about me must happen. Everything written about me in the Law of Moses, the Prophets and the Psalms must come true."

Then he opened their minds so they could understand the Scriptures. He told them, "This is what is written. The Christ will suffer. He will rise from the dead on the third day. His followers will preach in his name. They will tell others to turn away from their sins and be forgiven. People from every nation will hear it, beginning at Jerusalem. You have seen these things with your own eyes.

"I am going to send you what my Father has promised. But for now, stay in the city. Stay there until you have received power from heaven."

When the apostles met together they asked Jesus a question. "Lord," they said, "are you going to give the kingdom back to Israel now?"

He said to them, "You should not be concerned about times or dates. The Father has set them by his own authority. But you will receive power when the Holy Spirit comes on you. Then you will be witnesses in Jerusalem. You will be my witnesses in all Judea and Samaria. And you will be my witnesses from one end of the earth to the other."

Jesus led his disciples out to the area near Bethany. Then he lifted up his hands and blessed them. While he was blessing them, he left them. He was taken up into heaven. He sat down at the right hand of God. They watched until a cloud hid him from their sight.

While he was going up, they kept on looking at the sky. Suddenly two men dressed in white clothing stood beside them. "Men of Galilee," they said, "why do you stand here looking at the sky? Jesus has been taken from you into heaven. But he will come back in the same way you saw him go."

Then they worshiped him. With great joy, they returned to Jerusalem. Every day they went to the temple, praising God.

Then the disciples went out and preached everywhere. The Lord worked with them. And he backed up his word by the signs that went with it.

Jesus did many other miraculous signs in front of his disciples. They are not written down in this book. Jesus also did many other things. What if every one of them were written down? I suppose that even the whole world would not have room for the books that would be written.[3]

But these are written down so that you may believe that Jesus is the Christ, the Son of God. If you believe this, you will have life because you belong to him.

Chapter Notes

These notes include Scripture references. You can find these Scriptures in the Old Testament part of the Bible. For example, "Genesis 1:1" refers to the book of Genesis, chapter one and verse one. Use the table of contents at the front of your Bible to find the page where a particular book begins. The large numbers within each book indicate the chapters. Use the small numbers inside each chapter to find a verse. Some books have a number before them. For example, 1 Samuel 16:1–13 refers to the first book of Samuel. It is read "first Samuel sixteen, one through thirteen."

CHAPTER 1

1. The history of Jesus does not start at his birth, but at the start of all things. The gospel writer called Jesus the Word. This was a special term for God.

2. Moses was a great leader who brought the people of Israel from slavery in Egypt more than 3,500 years ago. Tradition says that Moses wrote the first five books of the Bible. These are known as the Law of Moses (or the Jewish "Torah"). The Law gave written instructions about how to respect God and other people. It includes the Ten Commandments recorded in Exodus 20:1–17.

3. Luke personally introduced his report. It was written for Theophilus, whose name means one who loves God. Theophilus may have been a Roman or Greek official.

4. Herod became known as "Herod the Great" because of his influence and many building projects. The Romans appointed him as the King of the Jews in 37 B.C. He ruled for 32 years.

5. The temple in Jerusalem was the center of Jewish worship. The priests who served in the temple were from the family line of Aaron. Aaron was Moses' brother and the first high priest of Israel.

6. Elijah was an important Jewish prophet who lived about 900 years before Jesus. Prophets brought messages from God to the people. The message was often about future events.

7. David was a shepherd boy who became the most famous Jewish king. He ruled Israel about 3,000 years ago. You can read about how God chose David to be king in 1 Samuel 16:1–13.

8. The name Jesus comes from the Greek translation of the name Joshua. This was a popular Jewish name. It means the Lord saves.

9. Abraham lived about 4,000 years ago. He is the ancestor of both the Jewish and Arabic people. Three of the world's major religions—Judaism, Islam and Christianity—come from his descendants. You can learn more about Abraham in Genesis 12—25.

CHAPTER 2

1. Isaiah 7:14. Isaiah was a major Jewish prophet. He was alive in 721 B.C. when the Assyrians captured the ten northern tribes of Israel. Tradition says that he was sawed in half for speaking out against evil.

2. A manger is a box for feeding farm animals. Jesus may have been born among the animals. A stable, cave or the bottom part of a house were used to shelter animals.

3. The son of refers to an ancestor. The family line was very important to the Jewish people. Jesus' family lines recorded by Matthew and Luke are listed below. Matthew recorded the family line of Jesus through his legal father Joseph. Many Bible experts think that Luke recorded the family line of Jesus through his mother Mary. By custom, the name of her husband Joseph replaced her name in the family line.

4. Exodus 13:2,12. Exodus is the second book of the Law of Moses.

5. Leviticus 12:8. Leviticus is the third book of the Law of Moses.

6. Micah 5:2. Micah was a Jewish prophet who lived about 750 years before Jesus.

7. Hosea 11:1. Hosea was another Jewish prophet who lived about 750 years before Jesus.

8. Jeremiah 31:15. Jeremiah was a Jewish prophet. He was alive in 586 B.C. when the Babylonians destroyed Jerusalem and exiled the Jewish people.

9. Herod the Great died in 4 B.C. Early scholars calculated the year of Jesus' birth before the correct date of Herod's death was known. Jesus was born a year or two before Herod died. So Jesus was born in about 6 B.C.

10. The Passover Feast is a Jewish festival that celebrates the escape of Israel from slavery in Egypt. God "passed over" the people's homes while the eldest son of every Egyptian family died (Exodus 11—12).

CHAPTER 3

1. The man referred to is John the Baptist, whose birth was described in Chapter 1. He is not John, the disciple of Jesus, who wrote John's gospel.

2. Tiberius was the Roman emperor from A.D. 14 to 37. He appointed Pilate to be the governor of Judea and Samaria in A.D. 26. After

Herod the Great died, the Romans divided his kingdom between his three sons. His son Herod Antipas ruled the region of Galilee where Jesus lived.

3. Baptism is a ritual washing with water. John used baptism as a sign that a person had turned away from sin and had received God's forgiveness. He told people who had been baptized to change their behavior.

4. Malachi 3:1. Malachi was quoted in addition to Isaiah. Malachi was a Jewish prophet who lived about 400 years before Jesus.

5. Isaiah 40:3–5.

6. The Pharisees and Sadducees were the two main groups of Jewish religious leaders in the time of Jesus. The Pharisees were experts in the Law and the prophets. The Sadducees were the upper class of the priests. They accepted only the Law of Moses.

7. The title Christ is from the Greek word used to translate the Hebrew term Messiah. Both mean the Anointed One. Jewish kings were anointed with oil. The Jewish people believed that the Christ would be the greatest king from the royal line of David. Many Jews in the time of Jesus expected him to free them from Roman rule.

8. Deuteronomy 8:3. Deuteronomy is the fifth book of the Law of Moses.

9. Psalm 91:11–12. The psalms are poems or songs of prayer and praise. King David wrote many of the psalms.

10. Deuteronomy 6:16.

11. Deuteronomy 6:13.

12. Many Jewish people believed that the prophet Elijah would return to prepare the way for the great king, the Christ. Elijah had been taken alive to heaven in a whirlwind. You can read about this in 2 Kings 2:1–12.

13. Isaiah 40:3.

14. The priests sacrificed a lamb twice a day in the temple. The sacrifice was a ritual way for the people to be forgiven for their sins.

CHAPTER 4

1. Jesus nicknamed Simon, the Rock. Cephas is the word for rock in the Aramaic language that Jesus spoke. Peter is the English name that comes from the word for rock in Greek. The gospels refer to him by either name—Simon or Peter, and sometimes by both.

2. The people had to use special temple money to buy the animals for the Passover Feast. The money changers and animal merchants set up their stalls in the courtyard that was intended for Gentile worshipers. The temple authorities shared in the profits at the people's expense.

3. Psalm 69:9.

4. The Jewish people complained to God in the desert after they were delivered from slavery in Egypt. He sent a plague of poisonous snakes as punishment. Then he told Moses to make a metal snake and hold it up so that the people could see it. Those who had been bitten were healed if they looked at the metal snake as a sign of their trust in God (Numbers 21:6–9). The symbol of a snake on a pole is now used by many medical organizations.

5. The Samaritans were a mixed race of people. They were descendants of the Jews and foreigners resettled in Northern Israel by the Assyrians. The Samaritans and Jewish people generally despised each other.

6. It was very unusual for a Jewish man to talk to a Samaritan woman. But Jesus treated the woman with respect and kindness.

CHAPTER 5

1. Isaiah 61:1–2.

2. The Jewish prophets Elijah and Elisha had some extraordinary experiences. You can read about Elijah and the starving widow of Zarephath in 1 Kings 17:8–24. Elijah miraculously produced food for her. He also brought her son back to life. Elisha was Elijah's successor. Naaman was the commander of a foreign army. You

can read about how Elisha healed Naaman from a skin disease in 2 Kings 5:1–27.

3. Jesus lived for a time by the Sea of Galilee. This is a large inland lake in northern Israel. In the Bible, it is also called the Lake of Gennesaret or the Sea of Tiberias.

4. Isaiah 9:1–2.

5. A demon is generally regarded as some form of evil, supernatural spirit. Demons were believed to be responsible for many illnesses. Jesus cast out demons and healed diseases. He spoke to demons directly. Sometimes they spoke back.

6. Isaiah 53:4.

7. The "Son of Man" is the title that Jesus often used for himself. It came from a vision of the Christ described by the Jewish prophet Daniel. He saw God give the Son of Man supreme authority and an everlasting kingdom (Daniel 7:13–14).

8. Matthew is also called Levi, son of Alphaeus, in the gospels.

9. Hosea 6:6.

10. The Sabbath was a holy day. God had said that the seventh day of the week was to be a day of rest (Exodus 20:8–11). But the Pharisees made up many extra laws for the Sabbath. The activities they prohibited on the Sabbath included carrying loads, picking wheat or helping the sick except in case of an emergency.

11. David ate the holy bread when he was escaping from King Saul. You can learn more about this in 1 Samuel 21:1–6.

12. Hosea 6:6.

CHAPTER 6

1. Isaiah 42:1–4.

2. Apostle comes from the Greek word for a messenger or representative. Disciple means a learner or follower.

3. Some of the disciples, like Simon and Matthew, have more than one name in the gospels. Thaddaeus was also called Judas, son of James.

4. Exodus 20:13. Jesus quoted one of the Ten Commandments. In this example and those that follow, he explained the true meaning of the Jewish law. He talked about the importance of our attitudes as well as our actions.

5. Raca was an Aramaic insult that meant you are spit. Jewish people adopted the Aramaic language when they were exiled to Babylon in the 6th century B.C. Babylon was located in the region that is now the country of Iraq.

6. Exodus 20:14.

7. Deuteronomy 24:1. In Jesus' time, some of the religious leaders were allowing husbands to divorce their wives for any reason whatsoever. All they had to do was to present her with an official letter of divorce. A wife, however, was not permitted to divorce her husband even if he was unfaithful to her.

8. Numbers 30:2 and Leviticus 19:12.

9. Exodus 21:24, Leviticus 24:20 and Deuteronomy 19:21.

10. Leviticus 19:18. Jesus later demonstrated what it meant to love his enemies. He prayed for them as they nailed him to the cross!

CHAPTER 7

1. Malachi 3:1.

2. Beelzebub was a name used at that time for the leader of the forces of evil. It was another name for Satan, the devil. The religious leaders accused Jesus of using the evil powers of the devil to free people from demons or to heal the sick.

3. Jonah was a prophet who tried to run away from God. Sailors threw him over the side of a ship during a wild storm. A huge fish sent by God swallowed him. After three days, the fish spat him up alive onto dry land. You can read the story in the book of Jonah.

4. King Solomon was the son of King David. He became famous for his wealth and wisdom. The Queen of Sheba came from the region that is now Yemen. She praised God when she saw how much he had blessed King Solomon. You can learn more about her visit in 1 Kings 10:1–13.

5. Isaiah 6:9–10.

6. Psalm 78:2.

CHAPTER 8

1. In his gospel, Matthew records that two men came from the tombs to meet Jesus. Similarly, on other occasions, Matthew mentions that more than one person met with Jesus. The other gospel writers, however, generally mention only one person—perhaps the one who did most of the talking.

2. The Abyss was a name for the place inhabited by Satan and evil spirits.

3. Sodom and Gomorrah were ancient cities that were known for the wickedness of their people. God destroyed these cities by fire as a punishment. You can read about their destruction in Genesis 19:24–25.

4. Micah 7:6.

Chapter 9

1. The people of Israel wandered in the desert for 40 years after Moses led them out of Egypt. God provided them with food for those 40 years. Each night, white flakes of food fell from the sky. The people called this food from God manna. This meant "What is it?" You can learn more about manna in Exodus 16. Many people of Jesus' time believed that God would again provide manna when the Messiah arrived. Jesus' questioners referred to Exodus 16:4, Nehemiah 9:15 and Psalm 78:24–25.

2. Isaiah 54:13.

3. The Pharisees taught the people to purify themselves by washing their hands and arms in a certain way. Devout Jews performed a ritual cleansing seven times a day.

4. Isaiah 29:13.

5. Exodus 20:12 and Deuteronomy 5:16. This is one of the Ten Commandments.

6. Exodus 21:17 and Leviticus 20:9.

7. The Jewish people had strict rules about what food was considered to be clean or "kosher" (a Hebrew word meaning proper). These rules were based on the animals, fish and birds prohibited by the Law of Moses. You can learn more about the food laws in Leviticus 11:1–47 and Deuteronomy 14:1–21.

CHAPTER 10

1. Jesus' wordplay on his nickname the Rock for Simon is lost in the English translation to Peter.

2. The Roman authorities forced a prisoner being crucified to carry his cross through the streets. Jesus used this shocking image to describe the challenge of following him.

3. The Law required all Jewish males to pay a tax to support the temple. See Exodus 30:11–16.

4. Isaiah 66:24.

5. The Law stated that one witness was not enough to convict someone of a crime. At least two were required. See Deuteronomy 19:15.

CHAPTER 11

1. The Feast of Booths celebrated the end of harvest. During the celebration, the people lived in temporary shelters made of branches. These booths were built to remind the people of the temporary shelters used by their ancestors as they traveled the desert with Moses. See Leviticus 23:33–43.

2. Jeremiah 23:5–6 and Micah 5:2.

3. Leviticus 20:10. The Law stated that both the man and the woman should be punished. But the Pharisees accused only the woman.

4. The question about Jesus' father was an insult. The unusual circumstances of Jesus' birth may have led to gossip about his parents.

5. The religious leaders became very upset when Jesus said of himself, "I am." This was the personal holy name of God. God gave this name for himself when he spoke to Moses from the burning bush. You can learn more about this in Exodus 3:1–15.

CHAPTER 12

1. In ancient times, God had punished the cities of Tyre and Sidon because their people did not turn from their sins. You can read about this in Ezekiel 28.

2. Deuteronomy 6:5 and Leviticus 19:18.

3. The Levites were assistants of the priests. Jesus' listeners would have expected the religious officials, not a despised Samaritan, to help the injured man.

4. Abel was the son of Adam and Eve. He was murdered by his brother Cain. King Joash ordered the prophet Zechariah to be stoned to death. You can read about these murders in Genesis 4:8–10 and 2 Chronicles 24:20–22.

5. Pilate the governor may have executed these Galileans for rebelling against Roman authority. While he was governor, Pilate had to put down several revolts by the Jewish people.

6. It was commonly believed in Jesus' time that disease or suffering was the result of sin.

7. At night, sheep were kept in a cave or pen made of stones and branches to protect them from thieves or wild animals. The shepherd usually slept in the entrance to guard his flock. In Ezekiel

34:23 the prophet referred to the Christ as a shepherd of the people.

8. The Feast of Hanukkah celebrated the time when the temple was rededicated to God in about 170 B.C. The temple had been restored after the Jewish people rebelled against a Greek king who had defiled the temple.

9. The Law stated in Leviticus 24:16 that the penalty for abusing God's name was death.

10. Jesus quoted Psalm 82:6. In this psalm, the rulers and judges of Israel, who were God's representatives, are called "gods."

CHAPTER 13

1. Abraham was Isaac's father and Jacob's grandfather. The 12 tribes of the nation of Israel were named after Jacob's descendants. You can read about why God changed Jacob's name to Israel in Genesis 32:28.

2. Jesus quoted from Psalm 118:26.

3. Jesus had finished his story about Lazarus the beggar by saying "they will not be convinced even if someone rises from the dead." Then he raised his friend Lazarus from the dead! Other people Jesus brought back to life included the daughter of Jairus and the son of the widow from Nain.

4. The Sanhedrin was the Jewish council of elders. They acted as Israel's high court.

5. Several popular leaders had stirred up the people and brought punishment from the Roman authorities. About 40 years after Jesus' death, there would be another major rebellion. As a result, the Romans destroyed Jerusalem and the Jewish people became widely dispersed. For 2,000 years, the Jewish people did not have a national homeland again until the country of Israel was established in 1948.

CHAPTER 14

1. Noah built an enormous boat to save his family and animals from a great flood. God brought this flood to punish humans because they had become so evil. You can read the story of Noah and the great flood in Genesis 6–8.

2. Lot was a nephew of Abraham. Lot lived in the evil city of Sodom. Lot and his family fled when God destroyed this city. But Lot's wife hesitated and was turned into a pillar of salt. You can read about these events in Genesis 19:15–29.

3. Jesus quoted Genesis 1:27 and Genesis 2:24. Women at this time had few rights and were treated like property. The Pharisees considered marriage and divorce as purely legal issues. But Jesus focused on the spiritual significance of marriage.

4. Exodus 20:12–16, Deuteronomy 5:16–20 and Leviticus 19:18.

5. Nard was a very expensive, perfumed ointment that was imported from India.

6. Jesus entered Jerusalem like the king predicted by the prophet Zechariah. (See Zechariah 9:9.) The people hoped that the Christ would be a mighty king who would restore Israel's greatness. Instead, Jesus preached about the kingdom of God. This kingdom would be the reign of God in the hearts and lives of his followers.

7. The shout *Hosanna* comes from a Hebrew expression meaning "save us." The people of Israel used this expression to appeal to their kings for help. It later became an exclamation of praise and honor. The people shouted this blessing to Jesus quoting Psalm 118:25–26.

CHAPTER 15

1. Isaiah 56:7 and Jeremiah 7:11.

2. Psalm 8:2.

3. Isaiah 53:1.

4. Isaiah 6:10.

5. Psalm 118:22–3.

6. The Sadducees referred to the duty of the brother-in-law stated in Deuteronomy 25:5–6. In ancient times, this law protected the widow, her children and the family property.

7. Exodus 3:6.

8. Deuteronomy 6:4–5.

9. Leviticus 19:18.

10. Jesus quoted Psalm 110:1. The Pharisees knew that the Christ must come from the royal family line of David. (See Jeremiah 23:5–6.) But they could not answer Jesus' question without agreeing that David described the Christ as God. Both of Jesus' parents descended from King David. But Jesus also claimed to be God's son.

CHAPTER 16

1. Daniel 9:27,11:3 and 12:11. The prophet Daniel was a Jewish exile who lived in Babylon during the 6th century B.C. He became famous for his skill in interpreting dreams and visions.

2. Jesus' prophecy was partially fulfilled when the Romans destroyed Jerusalem in A.D. 70. The persecution of his followers began almost immediately after his death. Many Bible scholars believe that these words of Jesus and other Bible prophecies will be wholly fulfilled when Christ returns in the future.

3. Jesus quoted from Isaiah 13:10 and 34:4.

CHAPTER 17

1. Psalm 41:9.

2. In his gospel, John sometimes refers to himself as "the disciple Jesus loved." John, his brother James and Peter were the closest of Jesus' disciples.

3. Zechariah 13:7.

4. Isaiah 53:12.

5. Psalms 35:19 and 69:4.

6. *Abba* is an Aramaic word for Father. It was a name used by children, perhaps similar to "Papa" or "Daddy."

7. This young man is only mentioned in Mark's gospel. Tradition says that he may have been Mark himself.

CHAPTER 18

1. Jeremiah 19:1–13, 32:6–9 and Zechariah 11:12–13.

2. The Jewish leaders had arrested Jesus on religious charges because he had claimed to be God. The Romans did not permit them to put anyone to death. A death sentence had to be approved by the Roman governor. The chief priests knew that Pilate wouldn't think these charges were serious enough for a death sentence. So instead they claimed that Jesus was a threat to Roman rule.

3. A Roman whip was made of several strips of leather. Pieces of sharp bone and metal were attached to the strips. People who were whipped by the Romans often did not survive.

CHAPTER 19

1. Hosea 10:8.

2. The wine mixed with spices was used as a drug to deaden pain. Tradition records that the women of Jerusalem gave spiced wine to the people who were being crucified.

3. Psalm 22:18.

4. A notice of the charges was carried in front of a person being crucified, then nailed to the cross. The notice for Jesus was written in three languages. Aramaic was the language of the local Jewish people. Latin was the official language of the Romans. Greek was a common language of the Roman Empire.

5. Jesus cried out with the words of Psalm 22:1. The gospel writers leave the quotation in the Aramaic language of Jesus.

6. The curtain covered the entrance to the Most Holy Place in the temple. This was the inner sanctuary where God appeared to the High Priest. The High Priest could go beyond the curtain only once a year to seek forgiveness for the people's sins. (See Leviticus 16.)

7. Crucifixion was a slow and painful death. A person was nailed to a wooden cross with heavy iron nails through the wrists and heel bones. The victim was forced to push down on the nails to be able to breathe. The legs were broken to make the victim suffocate sooner.

8. Exodus 12:46, Numbers 9:12, Psalm 34:20 and Zechariah 12:10.

CHAPTER 20

1. Didymus is a Greek word meaning the Twin.

CHAPTER 21

1. This chapter includes some text from the book of Acts. Luke wrote the book of Acts along with his gospel. In Acts, Luke describes what the followers of Jesus did after his departure. The book of Acts is placed after the gospels in the New Testament.

2. This disciple is John, who usually referred to himself indirectly in his gospel. He identifies himself both as an eyewitness and the author of his gospel.

3. John finally refers to himself directly at the conclusion of his gospel.

References

The following references list the Scriptures from the gospels that were combined for this book. These references will help you to find specific topics from the gospels in this book as well as in any Bible. This book uses the New International Reader's Version.® But there are many other translations of the Bible to choose from. The four gospels begin the New Testament part of the Bible.

Reference	Page	Matthew	Mark	Luke	John
Chapter 1					
God is the eternal Word	7				1:1–5
God became one of us	7				1:9–18
Gospel writers' introduction	7–8		1:1	1:1–4	
Birth of John announced	8			1:5–25	
Birth of Jesus announced	9–10			1:26–56	
John the Baptist born	11			1:57–80	
Chapter 2					
Jesus is given his name	15	1:18–25			
Jesus is born in Bethlehem	16			2:1–20	
The family line of Jesus	17	1:1–17		3:23–38	
The baby Jesus is blessed	17–18			2:21–38	
Wise Men visit Jesus	18–19	2:1–12			
Jesus' family returns to Nazareth	20	2:13–23		2:39–40	

Reference	Page	Matthew	Mark	Luke	John
The boy Jesus at the temple	20			2:41–52	
Chapter 3					
John the Baptist preaches	23–25	3:1–12	1:2–8	3:1–18	1:6–8
Jesus is baptized by John	25	3:13–17	1:9–11	3:21–23	
Jesus is tested in the desert	25–26	4:1–11	1:12–13	4:1–13	
John explains who he is	26–27				1:15
John explains who Jesus is	27				1:19–34
Chapter 4					
Jesus chooses his first disciples	29–30				1:35–51
Jesus changes water into wine	30–31				2:1–11
Jesus clears the temple	31				2:12–25
Jesus teaches Nicodemus	32–33				3:1–21
John the Baptist talks about Jesus	33–34				3:22–4:3
Herod puts John in prison	34	4:12	1:14	3:19–20	
Jesus teaches the Samaritans	34–36				4:4–42
Jesus returns to Galilee	36–37	4:12–13	1:14–15	4:14–15	4:43–45
Jesus heals an official's son	37				4:46–54
Chapter 5					
Jesus is rejected in Nazareth	39–40			4:16–30	
Jesus chooses four disciples	41	4:13–22	1:16–20	5:1–11	
Jesus drives out a demon	41–42		1:21–28	4:31–37	
Peter's mother-in-law healed	42	8:14–15	1:29–31	4:38–39	
Many sick people are healed	42–43	4:23–25	1:32–39	4:40–44	
A man with skin disease healed	43	8:1–4	1:40–45	5:12–16	
A paralyzed man healed	44	9:1–8	2:1–12	5:17–26	
Jesus chooses Matthew	44–45	9:9–13	2:13–17	5:27–32	
Jesus asked about fasting	45	9:14–17	2:18–22	5:33–39	
A disabled man healed	45–46				5:1-15
Jesus and the Sabbath laws	46–49	12:1–13	2:23–3:5	6:1–10	5:16–47
Jewish leaders plan to kill Jesus	49	12:14–15	3:6	6:11	5:18
Chapter 6					
Crowds come to Jesus	51–52	12:16–21	3:7–12	6:17–19	
Jesus chooses the twelve disciples	52	10:1–4	3:13–19	6:12–16	

Reference	Page	Matthew	Mark	Luke	John
Jesus gives sermon on mountain	52–53	5:1–12		6:20–26	
Examples of salt and light	53–54	5:13–16		11:33–36	
The true meaning of the law	54–57	5:17–48		6:27–36	
About humility and hypocrisy	57–58	6:1–18			
About wealth and worry	58–59	6:19–34		12:22–34	
About judging others	59–60	7:1–6		6:37–42	
Finding the truth	60–61	7:7–23		6:43–45	
Story of wise and foolish builders	61	7:24–29		6:46–49	
Chapter 7					
Commander's servant healed	63	8:5–13		7:1–10	
Widow's son raised from dead	63–64			7:11–17	
Jesus and John the Baptist	64–65	11:1–19		7:18–35	
Rest promised for the weary	66	11:25–30			
Jesus forgives a woman's sins	66–67			7:36–50	
Many women support Jesus	67			8:1–3	
Jesus accused of using evil	67–68	12:22–37	3:20–30	11:14–28	
Jesus asked for a sign from God	68–69	12:38–45		11:29–32	
Jesus talks about his true family	69	12:46–50	3:31–35	8:19–21	
Story of the good and bad soil	70–71	13:1–23	4:1–25	8:4–18	
Stories about God's kingdom	72–74	13:24–52	4:26–34	13:18–21	
Chapter 8					
Jesus calms a storm	75	8:23–27	4:35–41	8:22–25	
A man delivered from demons	75–76	8:28–34	5:1–20	8:26–39	
A girl brought back to life	77–78	9:18–26	5:21–43	8:40–56	
A woman touches Jesus' clothes	77–78	9:20–22	5:25–34	8:43–48	
Pharisees say Jesus is evil	79	9:27–38			
Jesus rejected in his hometown	79	13:53–58	6:1–6		4:44
Jesus sends out his disciples	80	10:5–16	6:7–13	9:1–6	
Jesus warns of persecution	80–81	10:17–33		12:2–12	
Jesus warns of family strife	81–82	10:34–42		12:49–53	
Herod kills John the Baptist	83–84	14:1–12	6:14–29	9:7–9	

Reference	Page	Matthew	Mark	Luke	John
Chapter 9					
Jesus feeds 5,000	85–86	14:13–21	6:30–44	9:10–17	6:1–15
Jesus walks on the lake	87	14:22–36	6:45–56		6:16–21
Jesus is "the bread of life"	88–89				6:22–71
What makes people "unclean"?	91–92	15:1–20	7:1–23		
The faith of a Greek woman	92–93	15:21–28	7:24–30		
Many disabled people healed	93–94	15:29–31	7:31–37		
Jesus feeds 4,000	94	15:32–39	8:1–10		
Jesus warns about religious leaders	94–95	16:1–12	8:11–21		
Chapter 10					
A blind man sees clearly	97		8:22–26		
Peter says Jesus is "the Christ"	97–98	16:13–20	8:27–30	9:18–20	
Jesus tells of his coming death	98	16:21–28	8:31–9:1	9:21–27	
Jesus is seen shining with glory	98–100	17:1–13	9:2–13	9:28–36	
A boy with an evil spirit healed	100–101	17:14–21	9:14–29	9:37–43	
Jesus tells more about his death	101	17:22–23	9:30–32	9:44–45	
The coin in a fish's mouth	101–102	17:24–27			
Jesus talks about humility	102–103	18:1–14	9:33–50	9:46–50	
Jesus talks about forgiveness	103–105	18:15–35			
Chapter 11					
Jesus criticized by his brothers	107				7:1–10
The cost of following Jesus	108	8:18–22		9:51–62	
Pharisees attempt to arrest Jesus	108–110				7:11–53
Jesus forgives a woman of adultery	111				8:1–11
Jesus is "the light of the world"	111–112				8:12–20
Jesus says he came from heaven	112				8:21–30
Jesus says he was sent by God	112–114				8:31–47
Jesus claims God's sacred name	114				8:48–59
Chapter 12					
Jesus sends out 72 followers	115–116	11:20–24		10:1–24	

Reference	Page	Matthew	Mark	Luke	John
Story of the good Samaritan	117			10:25–37	
Jesus visits Mary and Martha	117–118			10:38–42	
The Lord's prayer	118	6:9–13		11:1–13	
Jesus condemns the Pharisees	119–120	23:13–36		11:37–12:1	
Story of the rich man	120–112			12:13–21	
Understanding what is right	121–122			12:54–59	
Story of the fig tree	122			13:1–9	
A woman healed on a Sabbath	122–123			13:10–17	
A blind man healed on a Sabbath	123–125				9:1–41
Jesus is "the good shepherd"	125–126				10:1–18
Jesus is accused of being crazy	126				10:19–21
Jesus claims to be God	127				10:22–42
Chapter 13					
About entering God's kingdom	129	8:11–12		13:22–30	
Jesus' sadness about Jerusalem	130	23:37–39		13:31–35	
A man with swollen body healed	130			14:1–6	
Stories about feasts	130–132			14:7–24	
The cost of following Jesus	132			14:25–35	
Stories about lost things	132–134			15:1–32	
Story of the clever manager	134–135			16:1–15	
Story of the beggar and rich man	136			16:19–31	
About forgiveness, faith and duty	136–137			17:1–10	
Jesus' friend Lazarus dies	137				11:1–16
Jesus is "the resurrection and life"	138				11:17–27
Lazarus raised from the dead	139–140				11:28–44
Jewish leaders plan to kill Jesus	140				11:45–54
Chapter 14					
People look for Jesus in Jerusalem	141				11:55–57
Jesus heals ten with skin disease	141–142			17:11–19	

Reference	Page	Matthew	Mark	Luke	John
The coming of God's kingdom	142–143			17:20–37	
Stories about prayer	143–144			18:1–14	
Questions about divorce	144–145	19:1–12	10:1–12	16:16–18	
Jesus blesses little children	145	19:13–15	10:13–16	18:15–17	
Jesus and the rich young ruler	145–146	19:16–30	10:17–31	18:18–30	
Story of the vineyard workers	146–147	20:1–16			
Jesus talks about his death	147–148	20:17–19	10:32–34	18:31–34	
James and John ask for a favor	148	20:20–28	10:35–45		
Blind Bartimaeus healed	149	20:29–34	10:46–52	18:35–43	
Zacchaeus meets Jesus	149–150			19:1–10	
Story of the three servants	150–151			19:11–27	
Mary pours perfume on Jesus	151–152	26:6–13	14:3–9		12:1–11
Jesus is welcomed as a king	152–153	21:1–9	11:1–10	19:28–40	12:12–19
Chapter 15					
Jesus enters Jerusalem	155	21:10–11	11:11	19:41–44	
Jesus clears the temple again	156	21:12–13	11:15–17	19:45–46	
Jewish leaders reject Jesus	156–157	21:14–16	11:18	19:47–48	12:37–50
Some Greeks ask to meet Jesus	157–158				12:20–36
The dried-up fig tree	158–159	21:17–22	11:12–26		
Authority of Jesus questioned	159	21:23–27	11:27–33	20:1–8	
Stories about vineyards	159–161	21:28–46	12:1–12	20:9–19	
Story of the wedding dinner	161–162	22:1–14			
About paying taxes to Caesar	162	22:15–22	12:13–17	20:20–26	
The resurrection of the dead	163	22:23–33	12:18–27	20:27–40	
Most important commandment	163–164	22:34–40	12:28–34		
Jesus questions religious leaders	164	22:41–46	12:35–37	20:41–44	
Jesus warns about Jewish leaders	165	23:1–12	12:38–40	20:45–47	
Chapter 16					
The poor widow's offering	167		12:41–44	21:1–4	
Jesus predicts ruin of temple	167	24:1–2	13:1–2	21:5–6	
Signs of the end of the world	168–170	24:3–22	13:3–20	21:7–26	
Jesus' coming again in the future	170	24:23–35	13:21–32	21:27–38	

Reference	Page	Matthew	Mark	Luke	John
Being ready for Jesus' return	170–171	24:36–51	13:33–37	12:35–48	
Stories of bridesmaids and servants	172–174	25:1–30			
The final judgment of all people	174–175	25:31–46			
Chapter 17					
Judas agrees to betray Jesus	177	26:14–16	14:1–11	22:1–6	
Preparation for the Passover	177–178	26:17–19	14:12–16	22:7–13	
Jesus washes the disciples' feet	179				13:1–17
The Lord's last supper	178–181	26:20–30	14:17–26	22:14–30	13:18–32
Jesus predicts Peter's denial	182	26:31–35	14:27–31	22:31–38	13:33–38
Jesus is the "way, truth and life"	183				14:1–14
God will send the Holy Spirit	183–184				14:15–31
The command to love each other	185				15:1–17
World will hate Jesus' followers	185–186				15:18–16:4
Jesus will return to the Father	186–188				16:5–33
Jesus prays for his followers	188–190				17:1–26
Jesus' distress in Gethsemane	190–191	26:36–46	14:32–42	22:39–46	18:1–2
Jesus is betrayed and arrested	191–193	26:47–56	14:43–52	22:47–54	18:3–12
Chapter 18					
Jesus is tried by the Jewish council	195–197	26:57–66	14:53–64	22:54	18:13–24
Guards beat and abuse Jesus	197	26:67–68	14:65	22:63–65	
Peter denies knowing Jesus	197–198	26:69–75	14:66–72	22:55–62	18:15–27
Jesus is sentenced to die	198	27:1–2	15:1	22:66–71	
Judas Iscariot hangs himself	198	27:3–10			
Jesus is tried by Pilate	199	27:11–14	15:2–5	23:1–6	18:28–38
Jesus is tried by Herod	200			23:7–12	
Pilate hands Jesus over to die	200–203	27:15–26	15:6–15	23:13–25	18:39–19:16
Chapter 19					
Roman soldiers whip Jesus	205	27:27–31	15:16–20		19:1–3
Jesus is nailed to a cross	206	27:32–44	15:21–32	23:26–43	19:17–27
Jesus dies on the cross	208	27:45–56	15:33–41	23:44–49	19:28–37
Jesus is buried in a garden tomb	209–210	27:57–61	15:42–47	23:50–56	19:38–42

Reference	Page	Matthew	Mark	Luke	John
Jesus' tomb is sealed and guarded	210	27:62–66			
Chapter 20					
Jesus rises from the dead	211–213	28:1–7	16:1–8	24:1–12	20:1–10
Jesus appears to Mary Magdalene	213	28:8–10	16:9–11		20:11–18
The priests bribe the guards	214	28:11–15			
Jesus appears on road to Emmaus	214–215		16:12–13	24:13–35	
Jesus appears to his disciples	215–206		16:14	24:36–43	20:19–20
Jesus appears to Thomas	216				20:24–29
Chapter 21					
Jesus commissions his disciples	217–218	28:16–20	16:15–18	Acts 1:2–3	20:21–23
The miraculous catch of fish	218–219				21:1–14
Jesus encourages Peter	219–220				21:15–22
Jesus promises spiritual power	220			Acts 1:4–8	
Jesus explains the Scriptures	220			24:44–49	
Jesus is taken up into heaven	221		16:19	24:50–51	
Jesus will come back again	221			Acts 1:9–11	
The Christian church begins	221		16:20	24:52–53	
John's witness in his gospel	221				21:23–25
The purpose of the gospels	221				20:30–31